Four Eggs in a Basket

Let's hope that none of them are cracked

Brian G Mc Enery

Self Published

Copyright © 2023 Brian G Mc Enery

All rights reserved.

No part of this publication may be reproduced, stored in a retrieval system, or transmitted in any form or by any means, electronic, mechanical. photocopying or otherwise, without the prior consent of the copyright holder.

ISBN: 9798870678368

Cover created using the Canva graphics design system, with a little help from the Canva AI system as well.

Dedication

For George and Mary my father and mother, without both of whom I wouldn't have the inspiration, or courage, to write about my journey through life. For Paddy and Denise, my two older sisters, who keep me on the straight and narrow. For my Mystery Cat who inspired me to write about my true feelings of love. And finally for Patricia, to whom I was married for nearly twenty five years, and who was the most compassionate person I ever met.

Brian G
December 2023

Acknowledgement

I would like to acknowledge those who supported the publication of my poetry through contributing to my GoFundMe campaign.

About the Author

Brian G Mc Enery is a former army officer and served with the Irish Army in Lebanon. He holds a PhD in computation from University College Cork and worked for many years integrating modern computation with vedic computation. He is also a writer and poet, and writes both in Irish and English.

Contacts

Email: mcenerybriang@gmail.com

Mobile: +353-89-4042306

Preface

It takes four eggs to make a good omelette and I have included four eggs in this book. Each of the eggs is a smaller collection of poems composed at different times from early 2000 to 2019. There is a certain logic to the poems as they are included more or less in the sequence that they were written, but feel free just to jump in and enjoy the fruits of my labours. Each of the eggs has its own explanatory paragraph which gives a little more information on the nature of the poems included.

Contents

The First Egg	1
Plainstalking	3
Mend It	5
EEC Blues	7
The Last Few Years	8
What is Life?	9
Terrible Euros	11
Yellow Pastel	13
Written at 2:50 a.m.	15
Farm Pyre	16
View From Seeming Reality	18
University Challenge	20
Not Words on Non-Words	22
A Singular View of Heaven	24
Lines to Science	26
Conjured on a Morning	27
Honey Money for Science	28
A War Instead	30
Deaf Ear	31
Money Motion	32

Life's Breath	33
We too have known the grief	34
A word or two forsooth	35
Vague Words of Light	36
Nowords	37
To Balance so few a View	38
A Sound Pencil	39
Sounds Abound Around	40
A fly to die for	41
Not so sure	42
Heaven's Road	43
Poetry Knows	44
Duality is Important	45
Simple Lunch	47
Clergy of Democracy	48
Night Tremors	49
Nectar of Life	50
A Lone Road	51
The first taste of language	52
Friends of Childhood	54
From Son to Son	57
The Navigator	58
Stone Sentinel	60

A Limerick Man	62
My Corner	63
Seed Show	64
Night Before a Day of Light	66
The End of Dissension	70
End of a Political Hero	72
A Dawn for Heaven's Delight	73
For Consideration of Humanity	75
The Knot Man	78
Good Bye Agreement	80
Prison Garden	81
A Worthy Prize	82
A Top I Fly	83
The Second Egg	**87**
Kerry Light	89
A Spiritual Warrior	91
Kingdom Come	92
Making Camp	94
Tachyon Thinking	97
Knowledge Lake	98
Loch a Dún	100
Winter Milk	101
Flower Girls	103

Women's Touch	104
Tears for a Hero	105
High Hill in Wales	106
Wherein Lies the Truth	107
The King of Freedom	108
A Good Start	109
Calming the Storm	110
A Prayer to Mother Goddess	111
Healing Chant	112
Soul Work	113
A Call to Change	114
Looping Journeys	115
Knowledge Revolution	116
A Fool's Day	117
Dreaming in Heaven	118
After the Fair	119
Kenmare Gathering	120
Gold Foretold	122
Heaven Sent Falls	123
Be Brave my King	124
Magic Light	126
Trees of Knowledge	128
Warrior Queen	129

The Blue Loo	130
Roman Queen	131
Heaven Again	132
Healing Our Country	133
Mountain Memory	134
Leaving the Past Behind	136
The Road to Freedom	137
To Accept a Challenge	138
Secret Lover	139
Mountain Grace	140
On the Road	142
A God Calling from on High	143
Daily Space	144
Knowledge Emerges	145
God's Delight	146
Searching the Sea	147
A Journey For To Make	148
Holy Island	149
Exposing Truth	150
A Reason for Flight	151
A Blanket of Knowledge	152
Winking Mills	153
Soul Mary	154

A Simple Session	155
Food from Heaven	156
My Island	157
The Third Egg	**159**
I Dream with Thee	161
Dissolving Ignorance	162
Soul Friend	164
Waiting	166
The War of Words	168
The Power to Change	171
Rising to the Challenge	173
Let's Make Friends	175
My Krishna	177
What a Place to Find You	179
Planning Action	182
Soul Message	183
Dreaming Heaven	184
Eternal Gift	185
Playing Tiddlywinks	189
The Hero of the Hour	191
The Nature of the Cat	194
Three Simple Words	196
Let's Go Higher	203

Closing the Gap	204
To Teach a Thing or Two	206
Changing Times	209
Smiling Inside	211
Winning the War	212
Night Moves	213
Decisive Action	214
A Simple Life	216
Sole Warrior	217
Night Love	218
Chasing Ephemeral Life	219
Queen of Beauty	220
Queen of the Free	221
Pleading to a Queen	222
Tachyon Queen	225
Sea Queen	227
Snow Queen	230
Queen of Light	231
Eternal Queen	233
When All is Said and Done	234
Queen of the Night	236
The Fourth Egg	**239**
Death's Quandary	241

Seeking Signs	242
God's Plan	243
Unrequited Love	244
Crosswords	245
Shoptalk	246
Shadowlands	247
Keep Smiling	248
Favourite Place	250
Too Soon	251
A Listening Job	252
Encircling Ireland	253
Non-Jury Trial	255
Warm Friends	256
A Conversation	257
The Poetics Of Language	258
Opening Up	259
Struggling Through	260
Confusion Reigns Supreme	261
Light A Penny Candle	262
A Mother's Love	263
Warrior Lady	264
Simple Sums	265
Mountain Glory	267

Citronella	268
Inner Music	269
Before Your Time	270
Take It Easy	271
A Song Of Loss	272
Heed Advice	273
Foot Sore	274
Heartstrong	275
Bereft Of Fun	277
Beaming Words	278
Forgive Me My Love	279
Blocked Words	280
The Loss Of Love	281
A Reluctant Ear	282
A Scottish Journey	283
A Spiritual Gem	285
Nature's Love	286
A Common Passing	287
Christmas Lights	288
Taking A Long View	289
Conflicting Tendencies	290
An Emotional Edifice	291
Scattered To The Wind	292

Sunday Dinner Service	293
An Island Dance	294
Empty Hours	295
Early Morning Blues	296
Searching For You	297
Confusion Reigns	298
Thunder Mountain	299
Stilted Words	300
A Passion Of Words	301
An Emblem Of Birth	303
Stranger My Love	304
Hidden Places	305
Long Winter's March	307
The Loss Of Innocence	309
Memories Of Love	310
The End Of Loss	311
A Simple Life	312
Cloud Dancer	313
Getting Bye	314
Cosmic Influence	315
Imperfection	316
Forgive Me A Sinner	317
A Culpable Life	318

University Of Compassion	319
Scribble Scrabble	321
Burning Brightly In The Night	322
A Longing Heart	323
An Angelic Being	324
Universal Journey	325
Keeping Things Private	326
Dawn Yawn	327
Writing Thoughts Of Love	328
The Long Road To Nowhere	329
Come Back To Me My Love	330
A Peeking Concentration	331
Gathering Dust	332
It's A Boy	333
Time Flies	334
Mixed Messages	335
Moving On	336
A Loving Wife	337
To Sleep or Rest	338
The End Of Dreams	339
Memories Of You	340
Fulfilling Desire	341
Heaven's Door	342

A Rich Man	343
Ageless Girl	344
A Cosmic Marriage	345
A Journey To Heaven	346
A Faint Memory	347
A Melody Of Love	348
A Deep Kingdom	349
When Dreams Won't Come	350
The Price Of Love	351
You Are Gone From Us	352
Eternal Memory	353
Lost Letters	354
Just A Memory	355
A Monument To Life	356
More Memories Of You	357
Faint Words Of Love	358
Last Words In Verse	359

The First Egg

For George and Mary

Folding the Branches

Explorations in science, technology, politics and life

The poems in this collection were originally published in a dual language book, '*Faiteadh na Gabhláin* - Folding the Branches,' in 2002, which was printed on midwinter's day 2010 with the help of my mother's legacy. This current collection only contains the English language poems and are on the topics of science, technology, politics and life in general.

Plainstalking

I remember one night
late
in nineteen eighty eight.
A voice appeared in my awareness
which,
I have never forgotten.

A voice reflecting the universal memory
of words
without faces.
A voice of silence,
solitude
expressed in every breath.

Of the thousands who have had their say,
this
is the only one whom I remember.
In my soul you will find the record
of this
red man talking,
on radio,
a Navajo,
I don't know.

But he touched me,
so gently.

Oh! How I would love to belong
to his nation.

A rare beauty from this RTÉ station.

Mend It

I went to the Levant with
a vainglorious aspiration
with a heart full of hope
to do my part, in
saving the world.

The reality was different.

In a world not wishing to be saved
saviours become mingy men,
the mingy is king
of a saviours aspiration.

Bring home a good TV, booze, a stereo
that is all importance,
don't mind about world peace.

Peace has become to good a business
for it to be self realised.
Peace brings normality, and normality
is the end of exploitation,
so who really wants it.

To aspire to peace is the business of politics,
the politics of business is to sell the means
to promise

to destroy
the enemy.

That makes good business sense.

Destroy the world in order to save it
destroy it in order to save it from self immolation.
Destroy individual self-expression
in order to establish
what?

EEC Blues

You danced when the wall tumbled
amid joy
proclaiming your self-righteous superiority
the victory of democracy over communism.
But how long has it taken for this
dance of consumerism
to reveal, its own tyranny.

A tyranny I detected then
as the wall fell
and all seemed well.

Now we can see the extent of your tyranny.
Now we can see the extent of our lunacy.
Now we can see the extent of the apathy
    which sweeps through out lives
    which lives in our hives
    of working conditions.

However, you have become the drone
the moan
the groan
under the weight of our enormous
complacency.

The Last Few Years

And now it is time to write
on the wrongs due done by might
how many men in meetings den
continue with the fight
and stay to keep the channels clear
for flowing muskets bombs and fear.

Not now you think do I refer
to yesterday, tomorrow never
for all at once do we recite
that peace can use the right of might
to further all political aims
and so ensure commercial gains.

But let us say what's must be said
there is no justice for the dead
and when you men in prissy suits
roll out the men in blackened boots
and claim that peace is on the way
because they wear a blue beret.

This decade last of history tells
of stories filled with funeral bells
how many times at night at six
have we endured a daily fix
of war and famine, deathly stare
all the horrors of despair.

What is Life?

A question which occupies much time
cannot consume but much attention
so large and yet
so little considered.
Where in the non-time of eternity
did we find our birth
right at the centre is the universal source
of our becoming
seeing
being.

Today if I look closely
maybe
I will see
once and for all, reality.

How I linger on the brink of truth!

Suspecting that this will be the moment,
I wait
I watch
I endure,
always making sure,
that revelation will not be missed
but it never comes
at least not in a perceptible package
but then it is not a sensory reality

which seeks
a form of recognition.

No,
it is self-transforming
from self to Self
small self Big Self reality.

Terrible Euros

Why must we submit to this yoke of mediocrity
the only way known to control the diversity
of humanity
is
to make us all a meagre reflection of totality.

The great hope is gone
eclipsed by a grey reality.
Grey days with smoke from pyres
umpires standing on the field
observing the rules of war
making sure that you kill fairly
and squarely boxing death
in the appointed proportions.

A menu for a good war has been tried and tested
and now the rules are about to be vested
in those interested
infested
with the notion
that there is a blood defying potion
to conjure from the seeds of war
a heavenly emotion.

Totally based on the words at the time
the promises are made,
all future generations are exposed

to the dim hypocrisy
of a political peace.

How long before we see that
they on bended knee
have slipped into a reality
bordering on insanity.
Not now, not ever can we rely
on the ability
on the mediocrity
of a Europhile.

Yellow Pastel

I used to feel the the pursuit of knowledge was
worthy of time and effort
evenly it inspired sacrifice
and friendship freshly discarded.

But recently I seem to have been persuaded
that all is not as it may seem
even on the beam
of the bridge
over the gaping chasm of ignorance
which now
assumes such prominence
in our world of virtual knowledge.

Everything is now a simple vision in a desert
like blue orchids
shimmering a reflection of eternity.

The end is to enclose within a bottle
the full extent of titled beginnings,
without as much as a hint
of the real intention
until there is little left
but to stop and stare.

Full stopping, staring, into that eternal reality
is a really good thing,

to begin with
or end
never
say
no
to
it.

Written at 2:50 a.m.

I feel that we are about to see
a major shift in the economy
no more on material goods can we rely
to send our sons and daughters to the sky,
but now we must assume
the responsibility to resume
an upward trend
around the bend
and quickly realise
among amazing sighs
that nature plays a waiting game
And claims advantage all the same.

A reason to refrain from
writing words at this
time, with or not aplomb
is that this
is not an appropriate time
to rhyme

Farm Pyre

As silence descends on the land
the end of the tune of life has come
to the farm, where once
a man stood proud of his work
but now all should be ashamed
that it has come to sickly this.

Men sit in their offices and proclaim
to know
the way to run the show
to make effect a change in all our lives
but now we must ask how
it all came to this
that health and harmony have been replaced
with the death of rural life.

They are not to be trusted
those who proclaim to know
the show,
for now we have evolved
a fundamental flaw
a greasy paw
to underhand, the cosy notion of control.

Again, we are faced with a stark
choice,
to select elect reflect and do nothing,

or to reclaim our enormous power
of attention,
and thereby realise that we own
the environment,
and we have the desire to create
Utopia.

View From Seeming Reality

Why do I not possess the light of my life?
Why in the fain light of this life
do I assume no joyous countenance
always looking from man to boy
as if relishing the toy I have created?

My mind is all aglow with heavenly snow
whiteness and innocence abound
but not a sound fills the room
wherein it is hard to assume
responsibility for all this.

None other comes in through the door
an open pore, like the wound of Christ
beckoning full communion
with the single verse of life.
Asleep, awake it make no change
to a mind to rearrange
flowers on the altar of heaven
where there is an all aspiring will
Godliness enraptured still.

The canon of this universal self
is not yet known
although the seeds are sown
to give full bloom to all our joys
even though we remain

boys in the nightly game
to capture a dream

University Challenge

It really came as a great surprise to learn
that ye men on chairs of knowledge who do sit
do not posses any.
Political manipulation are the tools by which
your elevation came.
My revelation was simpler
merely observation
at your obfuscation in the face of simplicity.

The greatest danger to you is my confession
that I know nought.
This is as it must be
for all the fruits of this seed I did once profess.
Fruits born mentally
computationally
to be the excitations of zero.
But you did not want
to know.
You dismissed my efforts with vain praise
hoping to erase
the voice
the choice
to question the source from which it all purports to
come.

None of you have held the innocence
which drives the mind to the ends of the universe.

All sit in vain satisfaction
sure
in pension secure knowledge
without a care
as to the lack of dare
you will effect in minds
which will secure the blinds of ignorance.

Arise from your chair of knowledge and dare
to resume the quest.

A simple request.

Not Words on Non-Words

What light falls dripping from these words
forged in the fires of heaven
which assume more power than swords.
If it be true then every syllable
raises up the dead which otherwise would fall.

However I know of one more powerful
than the word
a one from which all rhythms rhyming flow
so simple, yet unheard by most
it rallies deeply within
the host, of everyone who lives.

No syllable can capture the sweet
and powerful beauty where they meet
the unique propensity to consume
all that may assume a flavoured density
in this world of our non-existence,
that is the key
to see
beyond eternity
to all, that exists
and consists
of reality.

A flavoured silence has more, ability
than all the tasty words that, may
assume form on the tongue.

For silence subsumes all
within its own hall
of perfect selection.

A Singular View of Heaven

There is a strange insanity moving among
the corridors of scholarship
insinuating a belief that man possesses
complete and absolute authorship
over his own destiny
that no tribute or allegiance is due
to the higher powers of intelligence
which manifest in defence
of the realm of totality.

I myself gave scant regard to these
until my mind one night creation squeeze
and show what energetic paths there lay
before a willing subject of the way.
Back then
it seemed like zen
did crush the spirit in his willing den
but this was just a foretaste of the sight
which wonderfully visited the night
of day
so to display
the way, to fight.

Now I realise with all compassion
that heaven can fulfil our daily ration
and supply to us sufficient joy

to be our one and only toy
that soul enhancing
belly dancing
fashion.

Lines to Science

There are scientists who assume
to give us knowledge roughly hewn
from information fashioned with a spade
but the misfortune that they bring
by under founded promising
is part and parcel of their over zealous trade.

From these words you are aware
that for such I do not care
but I wonder where will all this research go
like a train around a bend
we do not know where it will end
what bitter fruits of progress we will grow.

Although my words may seem unkind
to those working most refined
I ask you to search deeply in your soul
for here you'll find the source
of knowledge fine and coarse
and so orchestrate perfection newly whole.

Conjured on a Morning

This morning as I lay awake
dreaming through the mists of Heaven
a voice formed from the echoes of the lake
and softly spake.

It bid me to relate
a message on the date
which fifty years have marked by in a flash.

Saying, now I know the truth
of love
it lasts forever and above
all it contains eternal joy
and in remembrance of that day
I do, I do, we both did say
the choir sings
still.

So on the day of every year
you've lately shed a little tear,
just close your eyes
and listen.

For Mary, my mother

Honey Money for Science

A scientist once decided to be honest
and said I do not know.

I do not know the truth of life
I do not care for all this strife
this is no way for greatness to be born,
no way at all for brilliance to perform,
grabelling for money
like ants
around a honey pot
of gold.

Sold
to the highest bidder
is the common sentiment today
of those who say
that they
profess knowledge.

It is now so sad that greed
the seed to bleed the need
is now a fundamental form
to be applied for, as a norm.

Greed which puts nice clothes on
is known by other names

but always now the end's the same,
research.

Research but attach no blame
for science is unpredictable you know
and a great way to make money
or honey
sonny.

A War Instead

Why do I wish to retrieve my status
as a non-combatant
in this great battle, being
fought in the trenches
drenched with the blood of future generations.

All the great wars are over
or so we are lead to believe
by those with tricks up their sleeve,
diplomatic bags of tricks
tried and tested, invested with truth
by the machinery of information
so full of elation.

But now it is clear
that fear
alone is used, abused
amused
to confuse the resolution.

No final solution to the illusion of warfare
is pursued, as such a lack of control
is not perceived
by those
who oppose.

Deaf Ear

Do you listen to your self existence
the daily persistence
of your self upon the vibrating stillness?

Every day you arise from nowhere
nothingness beguiles the sound
you are displeased to forsake.

A radio cacophony
the sad tone is the drone
of words masquerading
as truth.

Money Motion

There is today no season of delight
no paper wrapped surprise
no Simple Simon innocence.

For now, all is in constant motion
never ending financial devotion
to the prophet e-motion.

Life's Breath

There is a sadness in my breath
that I am tremulous of,
looking within its volumes of intelligence
I see nothing,
understand nothing
of the source of this laboured mood
this *uaigneas* in a mother's tongue.

It is like I am become
old, before time
my aged breath sees into life
and knows no more wonder.

It is as if fit for dying
but not yet, for I must still
complete this mission.

And do so with a slight emission.

We too have known the grief

Now I must return in mind
to that night, standing
after Sunday mass.
A churchyard, thick with people
whispering about the latest
bomb
to go off in Belfast.
I was alone and no one spoke to me
consoled me, for I needed it.
Why did no one
bother to explain the grief
the unbelief, caused by their deaths.
It was then that I became personally involved
and remain so, for it is not solved,
although
more than thirty years have passed
since the night
my sight was lifted
and I stood alone
questioning.

For myself aged 14

A word or two forsooth

I forage
among
half remembered thoughts

uncovering notions
and
potions to distil

some expressions
of
emotions long detained.

The shackles of memory
are released
by these picklocked words

clasping at the truth
one word
or phrase
in fifty gets the tooth of wisdom

the fine seine mesh does better
on the Moy
with thousands glistening every year.

Vague Words of Light

It is with some sadness that I renege
on the quest for illumination
of the vague source of intelligence in life.
A systematic knowingness can be determined
by due diligence given to research
into the universal being which flows
in throes of blissful exuberance.

A youthful passion, is the fashion
which is most accustomed
to this journey.
Now in the midst of life
with child and wife, does not
seem the time
to engage in this sublime
search for truth.

But abandonment of this road
to the abode of knowledge
will not be easy, for I am become
accustomed to its daily sentiment,
an expectation of the end of life
and the beginning of divine existence
for persistence against all the odds
and evenings of the light delight at night.

Nowords

Now is a time bereft of words
not many or not few
but too little thought of,
now we are lucky
if a word keeps currency
for a day or more,
now that words are spread
line in line with dread
about the dead who
have perished now,
somewhere in this sorry
state of life
we live
now.

To Balance so few a View

The old red bucket sits on the fence
listening to the Tims and Toms
who would have their say, making a difference
or so they like to have everyone believe
on this important issue
which we must all on
decide.

Endless information takes the place of normal
conversation
as talk is stalked for the opportunity
to shoot to kill
to yes or no
which is our only say so.

What matters how complicated it may seem
it all comes down to
balancing letters on a beam
three on one, the other two
so few.

A Sound Pencil

I find myself at times almost bereft of what to say. Nothing much in the realm of ideas except listening to this pencil as it strolls across the page with such deliberation. Not a puttable in words type of sound, but one familiar to all if you at all have used a sharpened lead pencil. Like anything, too much attention does alter that which is attended to, so now the sound of flowing lead is reduced. But a whisper of its former self.

Sounds Abound Around

One day sitting in my office
contemplating the conjure of imagination
a butterfly exploded
from my chest, into my head
so simple and clear, so obvious and near
bearing news, views
to fashion
with compassion
understanding,
experience of the immense
complexity of life.

Simple as a nutshell
if all in melody
a symphony
to orchestrate the laws of nature
duly lent us for now.

A fly to die for

Long summer days, an evening rise
expectation, no great surprise
my tally of small speckled trout
not so great to boast about.

As usual my father's will
lent to him a shaman's skill
to navigate the peaty water
planting flies assured of slaughter.

Now my time to tie has come
a fly who's black body
congregates the circles on the lake
a sure beginning of the evening take.

Quickly, I run to the tent and begin
whipping threads of black silk around a hook
hoping for a fish to cook
a sure change from worms in a tin.

Not so sure

I wonder where our lives will go
what future does it hold
for I am so bold
not to partake of this show.

All is wonderful with the day
the minutes tick away
to glow in the last ember
of a year's December.

Now, I do not feel
that all this joy is real
like a fish lost to the creel
spoken of ethereal.

Heaven's Road

It is not every day
I take this road to Heaven
passing by the wishing well
where coin collections dwell.

A few words with a stranger
at the gate, will suffice
to open at a blink
a realm more wondrous than we think.

Too soon after I have tasted
the bliss eternal
Heaven's vested in
I am drawn to walk again.

And resume this journey of apparent strife
until this light
of Heaven's road
beguiles me.

Poetry Knows

I play at this game of writing words
for want of more to do,
there is plenty a doing
not all to my linking
so I continue,
on my way
to play
with words.

Often, I do not follow their meaning
no logical connections spark
the path of
the flow of
silent speech,
just a sort of feeling
a temptation held within the mind
at the back of the nose,
the smell of poetry
or prose.

Then it stops
and all is done.

Duality is Important

Duality implies twoness, an energy to interact
two centres from which movement, action begins
also conflict.

Perhaps conflict arises from a failure
an in-ability to integrate two flows of intelligence
déachas dúchais, could be replaced with
aondúchais,
the singularity which integrates.

Duality is a real, perceptual unreality
it does not exist, but its non-existence is
hidden by appearance
often the apparent is stronger.

As the impulses of intelligence flow
they assume a diverse character.

The singularity of unity is broken, *briste, brí*,
as if to find meaning,
meaningful expression just for the sake of it.

When the energies meet, they are unrecognised as
one
further interactions take place, often violent
unless the source is lively within
then evolution.

Cuchullan and *Ferdia* were like that,
both sides of the same experience,
brothers.

The closer the duality, often
the more abrupt the transition to unreality
more violent transformations.

Civil war is callous.

True resolution requires vigilance, not avoidance
soften the apparent reality of duality
allow each side to look through
to interpenetrate while retaining
individuality.

Twoness can lead to threeness
in a natural way
a scientific way
a peaceful way.

Simple Lunch

Today I returned
to talk with you, with ease
so simple a pleasure,
to share dreams
to opportune schemes,
without agenda.

To go deep within the reality
of knowledge, and share the joy
of simplicity.

The complicity of laughter.

A simple laugh, a smile
honesty at the enormity of it all
and our place, so unknowing, within it.

for Colin

Clergy of Democracy

Let us not be told
like children who are so bold
the right from wrong.

You have replaced the cannon
with a common law
and are become
the clergy of democracy.

And yet, like days of old
you occupy
seats of discernment
in a chamber of dissent.

Opposition is your only talent
where silence would content
us all,
and manifest
a voice of compassion.

Night Tremors

And now I will tell a truth, my truth
half discovered in the night
as light shines on the momentary darkness.
A feeling, a moment of sheer terror.
Moonbeams crackle in the dust.
To awake and recall again
the memory is dim
in these hours of certainty.
All is known about this life
but night life, not so sure,
often to endure is enough.
No picture images to relate
just a state of pure feeling
often misunderstood, like a child
jumping with delight
or fright
at the unseen tremors of the night.

Nectar of Life

I dream to see reality unbound
a glimpse which underlies
but Heaven's door is firm.

A bee sees it all
in a flower, life,
purpose on a wing
a sting to end it.

Were I a bee
mellow in age
I could accept this place,
but I'm not,
and continue
from this to That
hoping for
your honeyed expression.

A Lone Road

Life is becoming a toil
the furrow sunk in the soil
knows its own end
but I am going 'round the bend.

Not now should I display
a countenance of dismay
for you all seem so merry
on the juice of the berry.

Seriousness and solitude I have
the lonely road is my nave
a long wandering road
going towards Heaven's abode.

The first taste of language

The stones have absorbed the truth,
they echo the ancestry
of language, and living. Keeping alive
in memory of words
history, uttering from every cranny.
Small birds know this well,
they nest in history.
Always but never leaving their mark
with a chance remark,
which inspires the stones to speak
to the soul
of a passer-by, who happens to record
the beauty of the morning lark.
This silent history of Heaven's glories
passed in stories, from stone to tone.
Records maintained in well kept fields
tended by walls of inspiration.

Looking into a sea so clear,
waves thundering their crystals of light
so bright to make the heart thirst
for immersion.
Cold always at this time of year
but inviting Heaven to take hold,
unfold its supreme Self
in this old stone landscape

where knowledge echoes.
The progeny of walls, built
in silent contemplation.

You sit there beyond a brief expanse
brooding,
your stillness,
beckoning to my silence.

After a visit to Coumineoul

Friends of Childhood

I walked last evening
to the land of youth
being led by my dad,
for I was unsure. Slowly
and quietly
my stillness intact
I entered the silence of memory.

The names of the places
mixed up with the faces
eleven again I beheld,
the trees where once
we had our camp
had recently been felled.

I was unsure
as I walked
slowly.

Up the hill
which I raced down
fell down
as a boy.

Now as a man
I had become my dad,
gently, bringing back to memory

the thoughts
the feelings of life
when we were young
and lived wild, among trees
horses dogs crows
the sounds, the stillness of life
beautifully experienced
wildly transcribed
in memory
of long days
running
wildly running
caring for nothing, but
cowboys
indians
camps
tree-houses
and food quickly gulped down
to resume the play of our part
in the heart of life
down the lane at the top
of Ballyard.

Memories hidden by years
come back to be
re-cognised
as friends
and bring with them

names and faces
friends of childhood.

From Son to Son

Dad
I'm back now again
a small boy
just seven or eight
with my favourite teddy
going out on a date.

Your look said it all
your voice it was shrill
just whistling your tunes
way up on the hill.

Now that I know
what it means to be you
my son is a fine example,
of all the things
you taught me to do
being a dad is the one
that is true.

for Eoghan

The Navigator

Back again I sleep on this Giant,
among mountains,
where holy men once sat
in silent meditation
praising life
lived for a great creator.

Now the valleys
and ridges ring quiet,
full with years of
silent contemplation.

Once, however, for me
it was not like that.

Alone on a high ridge
above the saint's road
I crawled, on hand and knee
not to pray
but to survive, the ferocity
of a sudden June storm
which swept in quietly
and viciously from
a west hidden by the high
peak.

This most beautiful mountain
where saints still come
to pray, to prepare
for a long journey,
just like it's namesake
who journeyed perilous
waters to a new Eden
and earned the title of
'The Navigator.'

for Mt. Brandon in West Kerry

Stone Sentinel

high on the pass
between *Mas a Tiompáin* and *Piaras*
stands alone
but never lonely
a solitary figure
bedecked
with symbols of ancient lore

this stone sentinel
guards the entrance
to time
where Celtic crosses intermingle
deep rutted names
of the sunfaced script
bearing runes
for mastery
of His majesty

all year long he stands
greeting
the few who pass this way
knowing his eternal destiny
as wind, rain, sun and snow
wear away
his red coat

to reveal
the inner essence of stone.

powerful, peaceful, solid
always there when needed
always quietly dependable
like the men
who hewed those ancient symbols
which still have meaning
a thousand years
after
many travellers
have made
their final journey

guarded we hope
by another
so wonderful

A Limerick Man

My father could move his big ears
A movement that filled me with tears
At the sight of this man
And me his big fan
Being tickled to death with his cheers

My Corner

Wet and windy goes the day
As my head near *Feohanagh* beach I lay
Full up with talk of tender things
And tunes a lady sweetly sings.

Memories of youth rekindle there
Stories of a car with a wheel to spare
Now as I make my way through life
I'm glad this place beguiles the strife.

If you ever seek a place to know
The value of friendship simple to bestow
Just walk the road on there out west
And sit and sip *An Chuinne's* best.

Seed Show

Do you remember dear sisters
when we were young
the show of simple pleasure
we beheld
when out the window
in the orchard night
three dogs
filled us with delight.

An evening
on our own were we
father and mother
had tripped to Tralee
to see
the latest
movie show.

But we were blessed on that night
when dogs provided such a sight.

Our own home movie
so simple a pleasure to behold
for three siblings not so old.

And then like always
is the case
chaos descends on life

as we transform
in age.

But always recall that we three
once enjoyed our private spree
as dogs
one night
encircled
our favourite apple tree.

Night Before a Day of Light

I could really do
with a little more
purity in direction.
Although I am getting there
the road seems endless.
No telling where it will end,
no telling where it began,
just round and round the castle walls
we run,
and on and on
into the sum.
Beyond the limits of integration
into an infinite sun.

Now beneath the valley floor
a great and mighty door opens
underneath our feet,
revealing
the inner sanctum of light,
the opposite of night
where right and might
inter cohabitate
for all to see
the insatiable desire of man.

Beyond the ken of mortal men
there now exists a lion's den
with talon's sharp
and eagle's bare
to shoulder the burden of despair.
But down a steep and flighty stair
sharp eyes peer from the darkness.
Dare and peering
from out the blackened hall
they stare and light
the dark hall.

How often must we peer at will
and sacrifice our lives to live
as still men do. Not now
not ever in our lives
can foemen enter our disguise
and see beneath
the thin vapour of a half smile.

So little freedom do we now possess
that forgiven we would be
to redress this balance.
Great and mighty powers
now fight
to cohabitate the same space
within our soul.
No wonder
we lie confused in heart

and mind,
lieing,
lied to by all,
most normally uninformed
by only half truths
peddled by those
orators of democracy.

Now we are seeing its end,
but rising from its ashes
I predict
a new dawn of sovereign rulership
where individual life lies
no longer subsumed by mass tyranny
but stands alone in upright mastery.
A lordship long sought after
long forgotten
but half remembered
by those subjects of the royal road.
A way of fellowship beyond
the simple manipulation of information,
a way bound
to the eternal majesty
of true knowledge.

Knowledge born in the heart of compassion
lighting the way of mind
seeming to realise
the view

that Heaven is not a later place
but now
perfectly lived
a realisable reality of man.

Night before the first Nice referendum

The End of Dissension

How long has it been
since I donned the coat of gold
a vast perspective to behold,
now as I shed this shimmering fold
the loss of an old friend
could not be greater.

But it is time
to step in to the lime light of knowledge
and realise that the piety of politics
is no more
as we are being sold
a fop.

No longer do they stand for us
but bow before pretentious peers
who have created
a vast empire
to master us.

Now that we have spoken
to deaf ears
what is the reply
from the corridors of dissension
'never mind what you say
 we know the way
 and you must follow it.'

This is the essence
of a modern
European
Imperial
Democracy.

End of a Political Hero

What does it feel like
to be
apolitical
Just a few short hours
to see
a municipal
Election debates are over
for me
indescribable
the feeling of freedom
from TV
Unpalatable
diatribe and uniform nonsense
completely
unhearable

A Dawn for Heaven's Delight

I am starting to move again
the dark cloud is lifting
a little light on the horizon
a blue morning light
to propel the imagination
beyond
the horizon of today
towards the bright dawn
of a new reality.

Holding up a card of bright blue sky
God displays his majesty
when he decides to streak
dawn with flecks of gold
and pink
reflected from puffs of white,
resplendent in their chariots
pulled by white swans, soldiers
march to protect the realm of night

Tomorrow again I will resound in joy
at the new dawn,
I wish it could always be the same
the sense of change from night to bright
a light to delight.
But full noon becomes similar

to full moon
except of an opposing hue
we wonder at their dissimilarity.

Is there really any variety in life
or is it all the same old game
a moment of delight
followed by endless plight
the search for more simplicity.

Not that I really mind,
I understand the simplicity of joy,
not dependent on events
but bliss to be lived simply
every day,
and tasted with a being so capable
of reflecting
the full totality of Your kingdom,
an abode we can create
if only
we wish to.

For Consideration of Humanity

There are haunts of yesterday
in today's world,
a feeling of remembered times
as half baked words
seize uncertainty
to justify nuclear crimes.

The women held the fort then
and upheld the common cause
of humanity
to eliminate once and for all
a nuclear cruise insanity.

Back then I wondered at a plan
to alter the seeds of war
by knowing the truth that every man
holds within.

It seemed so simple in its way
to go where knowledge has its sway
and listen to the joy of life
a sure prescription for this strife.

So simple then it seemed to me
if we transcend humanity
and create a new Utopia.

Knowledge blossoms from the soul
of everyone who lives,
A field of knowledge
beyond
the personal view of life.

This is the source of peace.

But now again we see
constructed arguments
to justify
the powers of destruction.

Do not listen to these words of shame
which seek to justify
and blame
an unknown enemy
to create the excuse.

Now
I stand with humanity
knowing a truth
ignored.
It is possible to prevent
enmity
the root, the seed, of hostility.

For twenty years or more I know
that knowledge has evolved,

the field of consciousness holds the truth
the means to eliminate
war.

This is the reality
for our humanity.

The Knot Man

Ringle rangle in my silence
drowsing dreaming stirred
annoyance.

Answer the phone I said
grumbling on the bus.

Then
I hear a tone
to melt the stone
in my heart.

Friendliness and courtesy personified
an artist
a man of letters
lots of knots
bright with colour
childlike
beautifully childlike
with unstudied innocence.

I turned
we talked
with names exchanged
his,
a famous name.

The first windfall of that day.

for Michael Davit

Good Bye Agreement

There was a time once when we dared not hope
to lift the daily ritual of a well listened news
out of duty
ears bent
souls attuned to the tragic litany of
a province sundered by words.

And now it comes again.

Slowly,
inexorably.

Prison Garden

What seems like a prison
    can also be a garden,
Hidden from the harsh reality of life
    plants blossom,
Hiding their beauty, until time is ripe
    for their self-discovery.

The world outside seems cold
    to the touch of the senses,
But when we find our way
    back to the garden of youth,
Innocence abounds.

Do not worry at what seems
    to be,
Your secret garden
    teems
      with stories,
Awaiting, to be
    retold,
By you.

A Worthy Prize

No one should hold the world to ransom as now.
We must all,
be very precise in our interpretation of information.

War has changed.

Now is the time to act in the name of peace.
Peace means the ability to prevent, eternally,
not the temporary words
of those who have failed,
for so long.

Technology appears to provide an answer,
but as Alfred knew,
man has no wisdom
unless
he knows
his
Self.

A Top I Fly

The top rung of the ladder
rested against the wall,
looking into space I saw,
no one.

None higher than me,
and there I sat in lone company
with my thoughts.
Being perched so high
in a cloudless sky
gravity defy,
the thought enters,
I can fly.

Down, down, down I tumble
thud resounding bottom rumble
now to start to rise again
first to find a step.
A single step
a single horizontal —
with no name.
How to find that which has no name
how to see that which cannot
be uttered,
for name and form are one

entwined in an eternal idyllic dance
by the master of the universe.

At last I see a distant forest,
spires rising from a bushy floor
surely they will welcome me,
one who has made this journey, before.
But no, all are taken and jealously
guarded, by self interest.

Now I must pick up the twigs
and fashion a wicker work of art
the start of a new journey,
towards the sky,
this time delicately honed
by experience.

The Second Egg

For Paddy and Denise

Spiritual Walkabout

Recollections on walking, talking and writing in South West Ireland

On midsummer's day 2013 I began on a journey around Kerry and Cork, for ten weeks or more. I met with many people and had great fun. I found out many things which are mentioned here. Things about myself, about the innocent boy, about my family and who they were. I began writing and this collection was written between 3rd August and 21 November 2013.

Kerry Light

A darkened corner of my soul
Drew breath and energy from life
A living corpse was all I felt
Stuck in single sorrow

Then slowly from my deepest heart
There rose a single thought anew
A gladdening from within myself
A love I shared with you

Who has this voice within
Why does the feeling flow
When love surrounds us all the time
And darkened embers grow

Come down to me you said
Take up your pack and walk
Come down and listen to your heart
Let's pray and see the light

So off I travelled on my way
A nervous faltering step
Shackles carried on my back
Did gradually loosen free

A top a mountain in the mist
I dreamed of knowledge lost

The great tradition I came to view
Cú Rí, Cú Rí, to you

A place of magic in my mind
Where light does shine within my soul
The energy that you gave to me
Fills all the world with splendour

The time it takes to see the light
The time it takes to love
The time to wander through my youth
With messages from above

I thank you Dad for your last words
I thank you for your time
I thank you for the memories
The darkened well to climb

And now returned I feel refreshed
My soul with light anew
A single thought was all it took
A grumbling rumbling love

I love, I love, the whole wide world
My heart is breaking free
But most important was the thought
'I really do love me'

A Spiritual Warrior

Atop the mountain of my soul
I gaze with troubling face
A vast and beautiful kingdom
Dissolving modern pace

Slow down, slow down, and come within
You are a hero to the world
We fought great battles on this hill
Echoes rumbling still

Just sing your song and lift your heart
A symbol of great joy
Remember once the tidings
Of a gladdened innocent boy

These mountains you did leave a time
To wander in the world
But now your back with many tales
Sorrowful

I'll wash the grace within your space
And clean your heart anew
So you can lead the human race
To warrior's kingdom true

Kingdom Come

There is a light which lights my soul
A shadow cast by Heaven's glow
Darkened times exposed a place
Where secret joys do flourish

Forgotten for a time of life
No nourishing prayers do flow
But when the road seems endless
I step aside to pray

A simple prayer is all I need
A sweet memory of the boy
Who wandered long in to this life
Looking for Heaven

And now I know that Heaven's light
Can shine again in me
And help me to realise a dream
To live this life a-free

To lead the prisoners from the cave
To give them knowledge to be brave
To hold with grace and joy enslave
And show the way to Heaven's nave

So if you're lost do not give up
The time of light has come

The twinkling forest of the night
Will soon reveal a sight

A kingdom crowned with all of truth
Full knowledge all of life
A universal dream being made by man
This time, to God's plan

For we are God's most precious child
Creators of Heaven in the wild
From nothing we can sprout a tree
To grow the fruit to make us free

The time is ripe for such a thing
A kingdom of knowledge to forge a ring
Invincible life to one and all
Beautiful fruits this time will fall

So know that Eden's not a tale
But coming soon to you
And Heaven's not a future place
But our destiny, our human face

Making Camp

Near thirty years had passed in time
I wandered to this place
Good food for all us passers by
A kindly human face

The school is out but still there is
Great knowledge of the past
With stories from the hill above
It's time to break the fast

For Kerry talk is different
With questions always asked
Where 're you from, who are you
You settle in to chat

The nature of our being
Does hunger for this life
A country way not lost
A beacon in the strife

Five days I stayed within the grasp
Of my own spiritual home
And wandered high in to the hills
Remembering, I was not alone

For Mum and Dad had met down there
And so began my life

And beauty flourished in my heart
This mountain did it's trick

Two nights of joy I spent up there
Peeling back the years
Fighting through the misty night
Exposing personal tears

For weeping is a way to joy
Once practised not too much
Don't stay up here too long this time
Move on to find the boy

For he still wanders in these hills
His light comes shining through
So then I left with spirits high
And took a lasting view

I will return again some time
And do the deed I planned
Bring healing from this hero's place
And teach to make a stand

'Twas here that I began to feel
The courage now to say
That I'm the warrior king
Returned to let you pray

Away, away, I've been so long
Full tired, yet I feel so strong

I thank the people that I met
Kerry welcomes living yet

Tachyon Thinking

We think faster than the speed of light
The solidity of nature is but a flight
A fancy made in the mind of man
Not according to Your plan

Within the dream we can awake
A whole new world for us to make
Beyond equations of solid time
Our senses expose a beauty sublime

So delve within and find the truth
The riches of the world to loot
Not taking all, but giving all
This pallor of ignorance soon will fall

Computing beyond this realm of life
Occam's razor cuts like a knife
When all is said and done
Blindness be gone

Knowledge Lake

Around a lake deep in my heart
Just like a saint I wander
A naked man twelve hours of sun
Glory to God of nature
A way to pray come back to me
My heart is lifting in this place
Wonder fills my face

Then down across the bridge I go
'Tis time to travel on
Continue with my pilgrimage
To a source of love I know

My heart is bursting with a joy
Not known since being a boy
I'm on my way, my merry way
Just simply walk and pray

My sack it was not great at all
It ripped and out my gear did fall
For God's sake, time to take a break
And leave this ancient knowledge lake

Back in to where I spent my youth
A town that's lost and become uncouth
What folly did the planners do
Killing the commercial heart of Tralee

No matter, we will build a life
Designed with knowledge
Lost and found
Deep in the heart of Kerry

Loch a Dún

Up o'er the hill from Kilmore cross
I travel to your story
The stream does make a gushing sound
My heart with memories abound
'Twas long in years, with many tears
Since I did pass this way
But now I'm back, with a heavy sack
And days with you to pray

for my Dad

Winter Milk

With eyes of wonder, looking down
A horse clops softly through the snow
A brown trap laden
A man with a ladle
Fresh milk does smoothly flow

Wide eyed with wonder
My young eyes record
A memory
A time when life was simple
Silent flakes flowing
From the sky

Now, all of this seems lost
As I sit here in the Square I ponder
The cost of progress
The loss of simplicity

Perhaps nothing has changed
Just my aged perception
Makes it so

The children I see dancing
Around Tralee
Play uncomplicated games
Bubbling with life
Rich with the energy

Of nature's
Most bountiful flow

Flower Girls

Petals grow for you to throw
And proclaim the virgin queen
Innocence displayed in white
Our lives not yet entwined

Rose petals are a special favourite
Beware of thorns
But that's your choice
Everything in life gives us two

Her son was crowned with thorns
A cruel joke
Yoked like an ox
He carried the cross for us

Let us once again pursue
A path of pure knowledge
Love the Earth
And create Heaven

Women's Touch

Ladies light the way of life
A soft smile quickens my heart
I feel alive again under your gaze
The shy boy returned
In the body of a man

But you give me courage
To heal my soul
To dream a wonder into existence
To bring forth true reality

I thank you all for your gaze
I thank you
For being such beauteous creatures
For lifting my heart from sleep

Deep in my heart I know
The time has come to bend
My will to true power
And serve all
Honour all
Love all

for Maria

Tears for a Hero

A drop flows gently from my eye
My heart sunders at his memory
The days we spent digging for lug
Casting far into the deep ocean
Great days of joy long gone now
Our family camped at the back of Rossbeigh
All lost now in this prison Ireland
Rule upon rule thought up by plodders
No dream will be born on this beach
No fruit of silent nights to fuel the imagination
What are we doing to our beautiful island
What are we doing to our beautiful people
Enclosing public space
With tangled threads of EU law
Release us from this maw
You give me the courage to stand
And straddle the crack which brings such desolation
The fallacy of democracy which never existed
Except like now for a select and wealthy few
The blinkers of politics robs us of our sight
The chance to truly see and be completely free
The tear runs down my face with joy

High Hill in Wales

Climbing high upon a ridge
I gaze down from aloft
Fear grips my heart at the narrowing sight
The great mountain looms ahead
Ice covered falls gush from atop
Cramponed ice picks bring us in
To the world of winter
Fear dissolves with joy
High up in this fort of snow
A railroad to the top
For gentler folk
Crossing Crib Goch is a challenge
To remember

For Snowdon

Wherein Lies the Truth

These words are but a poor reflection
Of intended thoughts
Teasing a meaning spread in time
Continuous phonemes in a line
Linear thinking destroys comprehension
Intended actions never occur in sequence
Meaning grows in the soul from silent impulses
Waves of bliss bubbling to greater expression
Singing the joys of Heaven
Till all resolved we settle again to dream

The King of Freedom

Dreaming deep within his soul
The king rises to his role
To capture from those grimy hands
A beautiful people and beautiful lands
To return again a sense of power
That too much babbling has since turned sour
And lead his people to a better place
With bright eyes shining and smiling face
The dark clouds still have their play
But herald a lighting of the day
The time is nigh
You're ready now to greet me
And together we'll be free

A Good Start

A line, a line, I give to thee
To lift my spirit and fill my soul
You give me impulses in my heart
A bubbling reality

This sense of joy is dear to me
Clarity returns
The veil drops from my eye
My head turns towards truth

The search is over now for me
A long road was my way
Now to teach from deep within
And bring to light your beauty

Calming the Storm

The salmon leaps upon the shore
Giving life to your great lore
The players gather in the mist
A storm is brewing, the ship does list
A man of magic calls his girl
And dreams of memory do outward swirl
Then nature's spirit prances forth
A plot is hatched to break the court
We're led in to a brilliant mind
Compassion of the finest kind
The last great dream of England's bard
A living memory that life's not hard
Emotions gushing on the isle
Bring tears of joy to those that smile
The sea is calmed, the storm has gone
It's time for us to travel on
This journey through our life we make
Meeting friends for Heaven's sake
All trials are but a blessing
A gift to bring forth Your indulgence

for St. John's Mill Theatre Company
in memory of their wonderful performance
of The Tempest at Ballykissane Pier

A Prayer to Mother Goddess

Oh! *Danú* my love the queen of my dreams
Your body does follow the flow of the land
Your form is so gentle it captures my soul
And keeps me in Heaven wherever I am

Right now by this lake I'm safe in your arms
With cliffs all about and mist rolling down
The view is of Heaven and Earth both combined
So gentle your grace brings tears to mine eyes

I pray for our people
To learn that they own their own destiny
To learn that they own total knowledge
To learn that they own the right to peace and
    freedom
To learn that they own the right to true happiness

I pray to thee most illustrious goddess
I pray to thee for the strength to lead
I pray to thee for the knowledge to heal
I pray to thee for my love to grow
To encompass all

At Caumasatharn Lake

Healing Chant

Misty morning and the mountains reverberate
With the cry of a raven
A man emerges from his tent
And begins to chant
His intentions reflect and rebound
A thousand thousand times
Echoing back to the progenitors of his tongue
His clan remembers and are glad
And lift his soul
Then quietly he packs up his tent
Satisfied that the healing will come

Soul Work

To be loved is true
To love yourself is your due
Difficult at times to attain
Because of that stain
We all carry within

Cleaning out the soul
Is a worthy role
A job which takes time
Sometimes innocence to mime
If not attained then pretend

Fool the habit of judgement
Until bliss is Heaven sent
Then it becomes deeply felt
And all sorrows slowly melt
The soul rises in joy

A Call to Change

Egypt in flames and no one cares
Government has become the enemy
Of their own people
Peckish rogues in polished suites
Rule from above
Looking down they chant and frown
Democracy is dead
People are bled
For profit, by global disorganisers
Divide and conquer, cut out their heart
We're safe with our peskish words
It all started in the laboratory of Ireland's conflict
Let us take the responsibility to change
And bring peace to the whole world

Looping Journeys

A familiar face stands outside a shop
From Clahane to Killarney our paths diverged
Ken visited *Dún Aengus* on Aran
I tripped to the Blaskets
Island folk now
Quick words
Then off again
Looping through life

Knowledge Revolution

Within, within, within a faltering world
Conflict bubbles and boils
Contradicting tendencies expressed
The old guard have the power
Traditional means to suppress
Evolution now called revolution
But I sense a change of phase
Consciousness is awakening and spreading its wings
Sing the praise of a new world
A world of individual sovereignty
A world where shackled domination
Is replaced by the harmony of pure knowledge

A Fool's Day

Atop the mountain on the reek
The grey place was our ascent
Led by a warrior full of local lore
We stayed a little while to survey
From Ireland's highest point
Stories to tell of the invasion
Lines to recite, Ameregin's invocation
Dual language, the old and the new
Then down the ladder back to hell

For Con

Dreaming in Heaven

Clarity lives in a dream
Lucidity in the stream of consciousness
Which flows from below
The inner impulse of our soul
Pulsing with knowledge
Vibrating within itself, the joy of Heaven
For we are already in paradise
Although at times it may not feel so
Just new unexpected territory to explore
Uncertainty is always a challenge
But opens the way for our dreams

After the Fair

Morning light suffuses multicoloured houses
The fair day is done but people still linger
To chat, to banter, maybe even to barter
Their few belongings
Most have moved on, but I loiter
Another day. a wash day
The weather has cleared, thank God
Yesterday, fair day was a sod
Typical Irish Summer

The talk is about the weather
Foreign accents suppress our natural acceptance
Of life in Kenmare

Kenmare Gathering

Heading down to Kenmare town
We gathered from afar
A greeting we'd all had before
A chat in Murphy's bar
With talk of fishing, poaching too
We conjured up a stew
Friendships easily made
And faces that we knew

Then deep within our native tongue
We chanced upon a theme
An island race moved out of place
Dublin's follied scheme
A book of pictures showed it all
With happy smiling faces
The magic island of our tongue
One of God's most beautiful places

'Tis time for food I said to Jim
I must be getting on
I'll fix you up with fish he said
A luck I chance upon
So down along the street we went
Into the Ocean Blue
And then I sat and had a chat
A bowl of chowder too

Now off again I'm on my way
Up o'er the Priests Leap
With fondest memories of Kenmare town
Nuggets for to keep
The road is long the mountains high
I'm heading towards the sky
A beautiful feeling in my heart
I'm learning how to fly

This journey it is doing it's part
To lift my spirit, heal my heart
To be a human being again
To be a real man
To love myself with all my zeal
To hear the bells of Heaven peel

Gold Foretold

Spreading the light is my role now
Enlivening the spirit of our people
To know, that
Although dark clouds loom
They are tinged with the gold
Of a fresh dawn

Not all can see this gold
Not all believe in this dawn
Preferring to linger in darkness
But for many, a great many
Their vision is clearing
And look forward to
The golden light

Heaven Sent Falls

Tumbling through a furrowed channel
Sound gushes with ease
A thousand thousand years perhaps
Heard lately by man

The water falls from on a height
Bubbling blissfully
To be it, must be such a delight
Continuously changing
Continuously the same
Continuously echoing the
Rhythms of it's eternal nature

We can dip ourselves in that stream
And dream with its eternity
And so procure a little bit of Heaven

Be Brave my King

Don't create any barriers
My soul whispers to me
As I near my journey's end
I yearn yet to be free

Old habits bond within
And strangle my creation
The desire to lift the crippling yoke
That hampers our great nation

The time is right I say to me
To lead the warrior's way
Have courage in the acts you do
And leadership display

A whole new world awakes in me
Full knowledge's royal road
Our kingdom we can make again
To lead to Heaven's abode

Just talk and let the people hear
The plans you have in store
The time is nigh to celebrate
Ireland's battle lore

Up near the royal enclosure
The people talked of you

The man who had the knowledge
Our culture to renew

You heard the powerful echo
Of that most ancient voice
The time is fast approaching
To act, you have no choice

Fear is just a feeling
Designed to make you care
With skill you act from knowledge true
Consequences beyond compare

So rise my king and do your job
Lead your people out
From darkness to the creamy top
Just have a pint of stout

For that's the way in Ireland
We like to have the craic
Let's take the civil servants
And give them all the sack

Magic Light

A wondrous light, an ancient light
It is my dream for thee
Pure light enfolding pure knowledge
Driven by pure energy

On Dunmore head you lit the fire
Your oblation it was heard
It lifted all our spirits
And consciousness it was stirred

To act with truth and beauty
To give them knowledge pure
To grow with such certainty
That Heaven we'll ensure

For knowledge is the key to life
It helps withstand the strife
The entropy that's part of me
Designed to make you see

The laws of nature are benign
They love you all the time
But your perception needs a light
A wondrous brilliant white

So go within and find the source
The source of all you know

Then you will feel extraordinary
With a magical inner glow

Trees of Knowledge

The trees surround us with great care
They speak to us within
A message from a distant place
A fluttering heartbeat of love

They echo nature's bounteous gift
God's most wondrous charm
Even in this modern world
They fill us with great joy

Their knowledge of this world they store
For walkers passing through
A sense of peace and harmony
They give to us for free

So get on down the Beara way
And walk a while with us
The peace within you it will grow
Nature's eternal touch

Warrior Queen

I dream of thee, I long to see
You as your made by God
Your eyes they sparkle with a smile
My heart you do beguile
With beautiful poise you serve a pint
And light a hidden flame
Such beauty you do carry
With elegance and grace
A confidence I see in thee
A warrior of our race

The Blue Loo

Sitting down to do a bit
Of business on my own
To write a little in my book
With seeds of knowledge sown

I came upon a little spot
A pleasure to behold
A jacks into a pool so blue
NAMA would pursue

Then out the door I went again
Mackerel fished from out the fen
A chat with swallows in my mind
'Tis great to be of human kind

Roman Queen

The light shines in your eyes
A light of Roman knowledge
A simple thing that you bring
A Cliara you are my friend
A feeling grows between us
Respect for our domain
A warrior queen again I meet
And so happy to greet

Heaven Again

Yesterday I was convinced I was in Heaven
Clare hurling past Limerick to an all Ireland final
A few pints and chats
An easy flow
Friendship from the heart
Easily made
A drunken wasp skittering on the floor
Washing away my Beamish
Oh! How simple life can be

Today the last leg of my journey
Up the Coomahola to
Loch na mBreac Dearg
To fish a little
To pray a little
To be in Heaven again

Healing Our Country

The warriors gather in the glen
An ancient sound resounds
They chant with rhythm some healing lines
Invincibility abounds

Out from their midst there comes a man
Hereditary leader of his clan
A proclamation there is made
Echoes whisper in the glade

Full knowledge of this life he gives
With hope and joy this day he starts
Healing souls in all the land
Integrating all our parts

Mountain Memory

Again the mountains call my name
It echoes round the hills
And in the darkness of the night
A faint sound forms
I climb out from my bag to go
And listen to it more
When low behold the sky lights up
With full moon's brightening glow
The darkened clouds are giving way
A single star shines through
The white mare peers out from it's lair
And gladdens my peaceful heart
Then pay respect to her I do
And she thanks me with a smile
Then back in to my tent
I go and sleep the whole night through
From early morn a new day born
A fairy mist comes o'er the hill
And pours from up on high
Then out there peeps a little sun
Promising a fair day
And down I sit to meditate
A thing that's nearly done
'Tis forty years since I first came
To this place with my Dad
And twenty since I last did come

Full up of vedic knowledge
Now as I start to live again
And see the way for sure
I' m glad to come back
Once again
And think of thoughts so pure
For mountains are a healing place
They fill me all with grace
The greatest church that I do love
Sun beams brightening from above
Then off to fish I do prepare
And catch a little trout
You're a keeper I say to him
And cast a look about
This is the place that we did meet
A fierce and violent storm
A memory of our last great trip
A memory of the end of youth

Leaving the Past Behind

You have a very powerful memory
A man said once to me
My former professor from Galway
He knew me when I was younger
Such a memory can be voracious
It can eat you up
Gobble up your emotions
Continuously sap your physical, mental
And spiritual energy
Meditation helps to resolve it
To integrate the past in to the present
And thus prepare a way for
A brighter future

The Road to Freedom

Now down again from Heaven's glen
I ponder what I've done
The miles I've walked in to my mind
The searching in my heart
The joy at finding the innocent boy
So he can play his part
He's lived it all for fifty years
Storing knowledge between his ears
And now at last the time has come
To share his view at least with some
There are those who know the score
This country's rotten to the core
Politicians play a game
But for who's in power it's all the same
Mouthpieces for civil administrators
Is all they are right now
Suckling on a national sow
Pigs eat their young
Just as the state devours it's own people
'Tis time to stand against this
But using knowledge we can't miss
So if your brave and strong like me
Follow my road and we'll be free

for the Warriors

To Accept a Challenge

Now I face a personal challenge
To believe in myself
To have no fear
To lead with certainty
In these uncertain times
To know that from which
All knowledge flows
To open up the garden
Of my mind
To remind us all of
Beauty
The beauty of truth
The beauty of freedom
The beauty of a life
Lived in harmony with nature

Secret Lover

Back again in Skibbereen we chat
I was hoping to meet you
I was yearning
To tell you my news
The fact that I have found
The innocent boy
Within myself, he is there
Smiling with joy
Then last night we had such a beautiful chat
True friends
I won't mention your name
But you know
My secret dreams

for my Mystery Cat

Mountain Grace

As I entered the village under Brandon
I look for the house I stayed in
Thirty nine years before
A lifetime but also
Just a fleeting glimpse

Time itself may have passed
A little older
No more a soldier
Not of the national army
But dreaming of a new army
Dreaming of a warrior
To once again bring
Your plan to fruition

The seeds were sown here
Seeds of knowledge
Nurtured by time
A carefully tended garden
I could now feel in my soul
I was becoming alive again
The darkness was lifting

As I looked up again
At his craggy face
Another great mountain
Full of Heavenly grace

On the Road

The beauty of this life you know
You loose your way
Then find it
Strangers on the road
Don't judge you
They tell you of your inner beauty
They like to meet you
To greet you
As a long lost friend
A brother, or sister
On the road to Heaven
So get out there
And do your thing
Travel your own road
Deep happiness it will surely bring

A God Calling from on High

A beautiful place
God's own space
The hostel under Brandon
Sit down and rest
Mary-Anne said to me
Don't be too hard
On yourself
Take life with ease
And the search will cease
Just stay a little while
Next door is a good spot too
Good food, good craic, good chat

'Twas there I met Tom
A man of Brandon
A real West Kerry welcome
Although we just met
We've known each other
For a thousand years
The tears melt from my soul
I feel at home
Under Crom's home

for Mary-Anne and Tom

Daily Space

Out the back we daily track
The cares of our whole world
Daily decisions that we must make
Inspiring actions to take
Friends listen and chat
Never, not once, a spat
A virtuous space
A comfortable place
The Paragon of our dreams

for the Morning Philosophers

Knowledge Emerges

The warriors gather in the deep
Woods surround them
A glen lies deep within
Water thunders over the rock
A man emerges from the pool
Knowledge flowing
A stream of knowledge lost
Found again and remade
Recast in modern form
To storm the bastion of ignorance

for Mulinahassigh

God's Delight

A river flows from the source of power
A tower rises in the lake
Knowledge tumbles through the void
Bubbling bliss from nothing
Created with desire
The image of God
Smiling on his creation

Searching the Sea

Who're you she smiles up at me
As we scan the sea
Searching for spouts
Signalling the presence of
Dolphins or whales
Unfortunately none appear
To greet and cheer
A young ladies important date
A day for candles to be blown
Seeds of joy sown
Eight lights to glint
In a smiling face

for Freya

A Journey For To Make

From Cape to Cape the birds do fly
Why do they chirp at me
I'm going to miss the sea
But I must wander free

Then on across the ocean
With brightening emotion
I'll travel where the kookaburra sings
But I shall not forget
The friends that I have met
On Ciaran's island

for Mary-Anne

Holy Island

A morning light did soothe my brow
As I lay back down on *Cléire*
In again to feed my soul
On Ireland's freedom island

'Tis here I find a human kind
A fellowship of our race
With time to banter, time to chat
And friendliness display

A graceful living's had out here
With nature all around
A glorious Heaven sent place
A welcome you'll find too

Exposing Truth

Another beauty I do see
A perfect match for me
Graceful with a perfect back
I'd love to get her in the sack

To attack the bankers in their den
I need courage to say when
Expressing emotions deeply felt
Softening my heart my shyness melt

For honesty is a difficult thing
Tuning the bells of truth to ring
With soothing tone the daily chime
My hearts desire expressed in rhyme

A Reason for Flight

I just saw the windhover
Soaring majestically
Heading towards the sun
Of a sky blue day

These words may not justify his flight
The ease with which he spreads his wings
A prayer in flight
My soul to delight

A Blanket of Knowledge

Around the tables, out the front
Trippers gather to feel
Silence surrounding all our hearts
The peace of our own soul
A man from Cork smiles at me
We share a little chat
A wishing well he gives
A respectful little pat
With words of grace, he takes his place
At our most joyous banquet
And remembers the knowledge we do have
A powerful cosy blanket

Winking Mills

Looking out on to the land
The fog does hide your form
Offensive structures built on high
Hiding our mythology
Why do the build them in such places
Destroying stories and graces
I long to see you rise again
And tell us your old stories
For dreamtime is a way to sing
And knowledge our fathers bring
So disappear from out my vision
I say to you with much derision
There is no need for you at all
As energy costs will fall
You are a false hope
A new technology it will cope
Derived from knowledge new to you
But one I've found in mental stew
Now you're gone out from my mind
Thank you God, you are so kind

Soul Mary

Last night I talked with once again
A lady of much craic
A lady rich with native tongue
With laughter bursting through

I'll walk with you way out west
Don't start to early we need a rest
You're on your way, your own way
A pilgrimage to make
Your soul to remake

for Mary O Leary

A Simple Session

You'll have a cup of tea
Mark said as I passed
Down the road
Simple talk, greetings
We knew each other
But not well

Then over a cuppa we chatted
Talk of meditation
Talk of Wales
Simple tales of two lives

Then a few poems
Two poets sharing
A simple life

Food from Heaven

The beauty of truth
Is that it never hides it's face
There is no shame
Nothing is left to chance
It gives us a feeling of certainty
A little bliss felt in the heart
A soft glow of reality
A nurturing impulse of life
A blessed gift to the soul

My Island

I'm back again
A little bit older
Much more travelled
But I'm back
What a story I have to tell you
I've been trying to get here
For quiet a while
I had hoped to bring the book with me
But I'll have to do, I embody the book
An island that likes books
Three very famous came from here
One I listened to, gave me back your language
Now as I walk your hills
You fill me with grammar
You fill me with knowledge
You fill me with the desire
To be me

for the Great Blasket

The Third Egg

For my Mystery Cat

Queen of my Quantum Mind

Reaching out to touch a transcendent beauty

Inspired by a very special friendship, this collection of poetry explores the emotions, dreams, hopes and feelings engendered by an impossible love. Originally composed in late 2013.

I Dream with Thee

I dream with thee every single night
Never alone now
We whisper sweet nothings
Across space and time
Our thoughts traverse
A tachyon field
Instant messaging
On a universal scale
You and I are at one now
Within the field of absolute knowledge
Oh! How you have lead me to this realisation
The equation of life
The geometry of compassion
Expressing itself in simple friendship

Dissolving Ignorance

You make my day by playing games
With my mind
Teasing the truth out of me
The queen of my quantum self
Earlier I watched a male duck
Blow his conch of knowledge
Resonating with changing form
The solidity of the universe
Dissolving
As universal constants change with
Our perception of them
Gravity depending on the weight of our love
Soon we will fly to Heaven
And view all from above
The darkness of the valley
Soon forgotten
As we take to the stars
And remember our glorious being
A being once shrouded in mystery
But not now thanks to you, dearest.

You collect gems all day
And encourage me to play
A welcome relief from my toil
To plant the tree of knowledge
Deeply in our soil

A tree whose roots will spread
Throughout the known universe
You are indeed the universal mother
Come to wake me from my sleep
To fulfil the promises I made
When last our souls did meet
I say this not with certainty
For nothing is ever certain
In your realm
But I admire your dedication
To the cause so close to your heart
When I follow your hints
I know that we can blow the world apart
And accomplish the goal that I set
Standing atop the slab of gold
Imagining the world to be
Completely free
Of ignorance

Soul Friend

I see you smile within my soul
Winking joy into existence
Sustenance for me on this narrow road
But there is room for two
There is room for a whole slew
To travel on the path that I have made
I see you walking by my side
Bedecked in a flowing royal dress
Bejewelled with every gift
For you deserve this, my dearest
You looked after me
When I was lost
You showed concern
Your infectious spirit
Infected me
And encouraged me to find
My innocence
Let us be innocent together
Let us share this life
Let us go on into a new world
A world full of all possibilities
You inspire me to continue
And I love you so
At times it is hard being apart
But in reality we are always together
For I see your smile in my soul

I talk with you constantly
You guide me in hidden ways
To hidden treasures
You are so near to me
That all I need to do
Is put my hand on my heart
And I will feel your pulse
Entangled with mine
For we are one now
One being moving on a narrow road
Made wider by knowledge
For I have some, not all
Who can have all
I feel the caress of your smile in my soul
The gentle caring hand
Touching me so gorgeously
I touch you too with these words
Please believe me when I say
I love you, I respect you, I honour you
For you are my soul friend of the universe

Waiting

Waiting is the hardest thing to do
I would love to contact you
But I have said all that I have said
There is nothing more for me to express
I cannot lay it out any more
I cannot be more plain
And yet I am afraid you will not understand
My actions
Many will not
Many will think me arrogant
But I'm not
I'm direct
Direct as I must be now
For false hope she brings from across the sea
Hope which will distract from my resolution
I have waited a long time for the courage
To stand and fight
These monsters
With their weasel words
I know that I am impinging on your heart
But I have to be honest in all I do
I have to be honest with you
Most of all I am afraid
To lose you
Which is funny really
Because I haven't found you

I don't know where I am with you
What am I to do
I never thought it would happen
That I could be over the moon
But then I do, what I must do
I really need you by my side
A friend, a lover
My queen of the night

The War of Words

An eventful day in the war of words
No external words from you
But deep in my heart I feel you know
That my intentions are true
I feel better now
Earlier I was unsure
But I captured the educational system
Of our nation
That was why I climbed the mountain
Why I rose out of the mud
And proclaimed my deep love for you
There is a record of what I said
But for your ears only
I am happy now with my days work
Fighting battles is hard work
But I am the Warrior King
Will you be my Warrior Queen
Then we can go on to conquer
The whole world
And end
Once and for all
The misery of callous words
Used without care
Without emotion
Without our love
I see you looking at me

In my mind's eye
Oh! How I long to see thee
In the flesh
As God intended you
To be
Completely free
Free of worry
Free of care
Free to bare your soul
To the one who really loves you
You are smiling in my mind
I think you really can read my thoughts
Can you read me
Like a book I suppose
My mom always said
I carried my emotions
Beaming from my face
I wish she could see me now
She can I know
She would be so happy
I really do love you
I promise to be true
To all I say
There is always a way
To save the day
And pray with all intent
For something Heaven sent
I need nothing now

Except you
To give me courage when I falter
To stay my hand like a halter
To contain this unbounded exuberance
I have for life
And for you
To be my wife

The Power to Change

There are lessons in everything in life
Lessons which we can all learn
One of the greatest I learned from you
Create a diversion at the front door
Then march in the back
Today will have to be a quiet day
Quiet on the outside
But inside I will structure my awareness
Soul work today
Will you join me
Even from afar we can be together in spirit
Chill out for today
I have to wash clothes anyway
I have become a bit high
And not on hash
That messes with my head
And we can't have that
That's what's wrong
Too many hashed freaks
Inciting rebellion
But rebellion is not what's needed
To change the power
We need to change ourselves
Go within to the source of all power
Switch on the light
From within our soul

Turn our head away from the daily grind
Trust in God, nature and people
Trust that every one want's what's best for you
I know that to be true
To change the universe
We change ourselves
We tap in to that power
Which flows through our veins
The power of pure love
I know it well
I feel it
When I think of you

Rising to the Challenge

Today I arose with fury in my heart
The power to my computer was once again
Disrupted
But my cosmic computer is still connected
To it's source of power
It is forever connected
I had a little power left so I typed
My latest missive to you
Then I saw that we will not be alone
Playing mind games
Oh! We shall have such fun
I recorded a piece on the threat to the nation
No elation there
But I must state the situation
Who is the enemy of the nation
Wherein does this enmity
Arise
None other than the invalid State
Moribund like a cripple
Requiring a three legged zimmer frame
A troika of harshness
The State lumbers to it's final slumber
Then power restored
I return to the super-highway
Moving at tachyon speed
I quickly rise to challenge an

Entropic logical mathematician
To debate openly in public
The falsity of his perception
That there is nothing to be gained
From playing mind games
I advised him to be wary of me
Because if necessary I will turn
His false logic
And slice him open with Occam's razor
The sword of Damocles cuts the Gordian knot
And sets all the children free
Of this ratted maze
Currently called
Education

Let's Make Friends

You and I are great friends
You poke my mind in jest
Just to see what will pop out
It has always been that way
Some times we may not see each other
For a span of time
But when we do
I always notice you
Even though you might be busy
And a little bit, aloof
Your presence fills my heart
Today I made a game
For three
A simple card game
To practice making friends
With numbers
For numbers can be our best friends
Once not thought of
Too seriously
Like all friendships
Seriousness destroys it
As said in the Prophet
'Don't get so close
As to not let
The gentle breeze of life
Flow between you'

For we are all each and every one
A child of God
His one true representative
On Earth
We are all a Messiah in the making
Some still proving in a bowl
Some have just entered the sacred fire
Others nearing their time to emerge
As food for the Lotus Eaters
As for me
I'm the odd man out
The extra one in the baker's dozen
I don't feel or look odd
I'm neither odd nor even
Neither prime, transcendental nor real
Imaginary may be I am
Imagining the world in to a new existence
An existence which with persistence
We can do together
And leave a legacy that lasts
Forever

My Krishna

You know an awful lot more
Than you let on to know
Even if you don't know you know
At least within my universe
That is so
Now I know why I am so attracted to you
And always treat you with respect
For you are my Krishna
You are my charioteer
I always knew I was Arjuna
Ever since I first read the Bhagavad Gita
Maharishi's commentary
Over and over
I embodied it
Then down in the valley
I read it in Sanskrit
Not Devanagari mind you
I know it but need practice
What would it be like to read it with you
It's not that hard
I can show you
If you have forgotten
Then we would both remember
All our lives together
What bliss that would be
A hero and a heroine of the universe

Finding each other again
Perhaps my lady I say too much
But I am just a humble scholar
Overjoyed at a possibility
Of resolving a conundrum
The drum of Shiva sounds the syllables
And starts Panini's knowledge
What would it be like to find
Our equivalent
I have an idea where it is
But I need other scholars
To help
I will no longer travel on my own
The lone road is at an end
I have traversed it all
Now it is time to bring
The army of bird people
Home to roost
To roost in trees of knowledge
To roost and chirp and sing
The joys of Heaven

What a Place to Find You

Last night I went to the *Tínteán Ceoil*
The Monday night sessions
In the village
Where people from the community
Gather
To sing a song
To play some music
To tap a dance
To recite a poem
I had my book with me
My first book
I had intended reciting the first poem
Not in the book
But of Ireland
But I didn't
I noticed however a leaflet stuck in the back
One I had picked up
At the HSE's West Cork soiree
Where they exposed their true manipulative self
To me
An organisation fighting a psychological war
Against our nation
Full with external views
They smother the natural genius and exuberance
Of our people
Young people most of all

I sought to use it as a book mark
To mark the warrior's poem
I opened the page
And low and behold
You were there before me
Couched between the lines
Describing
The forty boons of our warriors
I could feel your pain
I could feel your anxiety
I could feel your frustration
At a system designed to diagnose
But without one whit of a notion how to act
I thought of you all evening
As I listened to
Music
Song
The chat
The banter
Of an Irish night
The difference to the worry you have
Travelling to meeting after meeting
Articulating your position about
Our deeply flawed
Educational system
A system now at war with itself
So what to do
I have to do something

Because it impinges directly
On my own work
So I moved on to the net
And set up a blog
Here we will log the stories
Of those parents who have been duped
By an excessively arrogant system
All of this for you
I was going to go up against them directly
But I need to gather the warriors
We need to share stories
We need to listen and be listened to
We need to gain combined strength
Then we can slay this dragon
Hurting our children

Planning Action

This morning I began a plan
An action plan in meta style
A style you are familiar with
At least a little
From your time
As a uniformed lady
In a while I begin to articulate
My view
My perception
It is not complete
It is from my own experience
Will you tell me yours
I know it will be painful
But my love
You will have to trust me
I know you yearn for action
You yearn for a solution
There is none
Only a process of resolution
Resolve to evolve to a new state of being
But the universe is dynamic
It always throws new challenges at us
We may find it difficult too meet them
But with practice, care and planning
We can forebear
And live to fight another day

Soul Message

You read my poetry
So you know how I feel
It was just uuuuuum
But such a beautiful uuuuuum
My little pushkin
You are purring
I can rest easy
Whatever you decide
I did right to write
Expose my true feelings to you
I will see you soon
Then we can talk
Oh! Such sweet talk
Not soppy stuff
We never do that
But to talk of things which are
Hidden in my heart
To share our innermost secrets
To find the unseen places of commonality
The duality of our lives becoming one
Of course this will take time
Of course we each have things to see to
But my love
The sheer joy at your message
Lit up my soul

Dreaming Heaven

Misty morning and the surf just visible
On Fermoyle beach
My father's waterfall not seen
I talk with you
Tell you my plight
But I don't care anymore
I know how to fight
I will fight to defend us all
From the crass ignorance of
Objective science
That's what this is all about
A mechanistic view which destroys
The dreamers of tomorrow
But we will dream our own reality
Into existence
And live in Heaven
For eternity

Eternal Gift

Of course she will like her pressies
They are of a special kind
A kind of royal beauty
Suited for a Queen
A Queen of my Heaven
A Queen of my mind
A lady I'm so in love with
That I've become her warrior
I fight for her each day
I take her quiet suggestions
Issued from afar
But now I'm going to meet her
To see her beautiful smile
She'll flutter like a fairy
And fill my heart with joy
I never knew I had it
This power to stand and fight
But you arose within me
Action without fright
I do it all for you, my dear
But also for us all
If just one is left a wanting
It will sadden my soul
For souls are not just in us
They spread out like a field
The field of love we do embrace

And so give to life our grace
So soon we will be one again
Embracing just as friends
Exchanging smiles and gifts alike
I hope you have my trike
For my royal bike, it's still in Galway
Fenced in like all the rest
The city is a prison
A prison bound by chains
Handcuffed to great ignorance
Displayed by arrogance
Personified by a lordling
A man of dubious character
Who destroyed a beautiful place
For the sake of that boat race
We'll journey there my love, in time
We'll journey there to free
The people from the bondage
The city from the scheme
For schemers are they all my dear
They scheme with envelopes brown
And do the dirtiest thing they can
A thing that makes you frown
But now the way is clear for us
The road ahead is clear
Although it seems I cannot win
I'm moving without fear
I thank you darling for your courage

It did infect me too
You showed me how to light my life
And build my soul anew
It's you I blame for all this joy
You did bring a warrior home
You gave me courage to stand my ground
And recite that warrior's poem
I said I found you hidden there
Smiling from out the page
Your face imagined in my mind
Filled me so with grace
But I felt a certain sentiment
That hurt you bear within
The actions that they take with you
Will drive you to distraction
But now they've one to deal with
And I will handle them
They will at once be occupied
With tasks I set for them
They'll change or I will fire them
From out their cushy jobs
This is one promise I will make
This path of truth I'll not forsake
For they hurt our children with their words
Of crass indifferent ignorance
This is the real pressie
I'll give you on the day

We promise to be
Together for eternity

Playing Tiddlywinks

All I can think of all the way up in the bus is you
I have made love with you a thousand times
I have washed your hair
Caressed you in the bath
Kissed you
Felt your heart
Sucked your nipple
Touched your gentle soul
I touch it now
So much is my love for you
I have slept a thousand nights
With you
Felt your breast upon my chest
That warm flesh that excites me so
I have seen you naked
And you me
We have shouted with the bliss of Heaven
Soared over the universe
Chased a song over the Milky Way
Out beyond the Oort cloud
We roam free of Sun's influence
Becoming once again
Children of star light
When we sit together
My mind dreams
An endless dream of joy

A toy to gladden the heart
An honest account of your beauty
Which has captured me
We are best of friends
And we're not playing tiddlywinks

The Hero of the Hour

Looking back over words written
Gladdens my heart
My desire for you is true
Even this morning with a mushy head
You shine through the darkness
Your pure light I see
Through this maddening world
And I am mad
Not at you, my dear
Of course not
That could never be
But I'm mad at them
They're forcing me to action
I don't want
They're forcing me to call
For military action
Hopefully today I can charge my computer
And then I will decide
I am so unsure of the road ahead
I'm not unsure of thee
Deeply
But, what am I to do
We need to effect a change in this country
Our people are hurting
I am hurting
You are hurting

They are hurting our children
With their callous disregard
For our genius
They hurt you too
Tomorrow, or the next day
I am both
Homeless
And penniless
No place to ask you to come
But I know it won't be for long
For I am the hero of the hour
I have the infinite power
Of the universe
Flowing through my finger tips
Finger tips which long
To touch you
To love you
To ease the burden of your hurt
And release
The tender heart you so possess
I know I can come through this
For I am the hero of the hour
And I have the power
Of the universe
That single line of truth
Which guides our destiny into tomorrow
And shapes the lives we live
Into our glorious future

I have fought hard, these past weeks
It is not like me to be like that
But I fight for thee
I fight for you
You inspire me to great action
You inspire me to take up the sword
And cut through the chains of ignorance
That so binds the souls of many
In reality I'm no hero
Just a very determined guy

The Nature of the Cat

I'm purring like a cat
Even though I have nothing
I'm so extremely happy
It's like the universe is finally responding
Bringing me all the good things
I've so long for sought
And you, what about you
Are you purring too, my pushkin
I have changed beyond all belief
My mind creates a new world every day
I look forward to it
To meeting the challenge of the day
And challenges there are
Last night a lady insulted me continuously
But it's like water off a duck's back
I know that today she will only have a faint inkling
I don't ever forget, but I do forgive
Not out of goodheartedness or anything like that
But because of vedic knowledge
Heyam dhukham anagatam
'In the vicinity of coherence
 Hostile tendencies decrease'
The field brings them out, but
They don't hurt me
I do defend myself
But I don't get angry

That's what I love about us
It never happens
It never has
And it never will
For I carry you in my soul
Some times I'm uncertain what to do
With you
You can sometimes be very aloof
Which is good
For you have such an independent spirit
And I can dominate
But you keep me on my toes
Please keep doing it
Please keep pushing me into action
For then, we will succeed
And create a beautiful life
For us
And for all

Three Simple Words

Back again in Cork's eight star college
I think about last night
I was going to contact you, my dear
But there was a certain fear
Not of or for you no of course
We hold our internal discourse
A way to connect from deep within
A way to touch our souls
You talk to me quite constantly
In gentle subtle tones
And bring to life my inner self
That's been sitting on the shelf
No, the fear was of my action
My reaction to their inaction
For I'll be most surprised
If they respond at all
What will I do
Where will I go
I cannot at all decide
But something must be done
Before global forces collide
For what's at stake is more than us
We must stop the bleeding pus
We're heading for a global war
I can feel it in the air
To stop this thing I too must act

That action now I know
A subtle bit of knowledge
Across the sands I'll blow
It was in my mind to tell her
This lady Farsi full
She asked for knowledge on the way
To use a beaming light
May be it will just drop a bomb
A silent little package
Enough I hope to end the fear
And peace's road to steer
I thank you for your inspiration
To quell my troubled mind
And restore the balance in my soul
You clearly know your role
To guide me from a distant place
To be my one true joy
To listen to the pleadings
Of that most innocent boy
For he has come out from his cave
He's turned his head around
He sees you in his glorious life
All radiant with light
For you're the Queen of Heaven
A lady of great splendour
The light it shines from out your eyes
And settles on my soul
It lights a fire within me

Sparks a kindle dry
It warms my heart with kindness
When e're I think of thee
I now these words are powerful
And I must use them with great care
Emotions that we all do have
Are easy enough to scare
So please accept this as a gift
A humbled humbling phrase
So used and yet not understood
Entirely on this Earth
I mean it from my inner self
I mean it from my soul
I'll say it now and let's be done
For I've a way to run
To run around and find a spot
Where I can convince that lot
That I have the knowledge
To end it once and all
To end the fear which faces all
The fear which drives them on
To do daft things upon the net
And conflict to beget
But they are innocent too
They mean no harm to us
They're simply acting in a way
To kick a global fuss
So what's the phrase I hear you say

What is the power of words
What can you say to one and all
That darkness it will fall
The age of ignorance will be gone
When uttered words are true
Three simple words I do combine
To express my deepest view
They are an expression of totality
From deep within my soul
They helped me climb from out the cave
And emerge in to the light
I will at once say what they are
No wandering 'round the world
They're said with deepest feeling
They're powerful and they're healing
So now my dear you must be brave
And listen to this knave
A man of tender loyalties
To you he does declare
I love you
But that's not all I have to say
There is another way
To heal yourself and dry your tears
And do away with fears
By turning back one word in three
And having inner spree
For then you will at once realise
You are a powerful being

A gracious kitten of a lady
I see within my soul
These words they have great power for me
They helped to set me free
From whence they came I did not know
But then I saw them all
Recorded in the deepest dark
A time of night-time pleading
Pleading with the lord of all
To lift this terrible caul
And free me from this awful cave
A dark and dankened nave
I had forgot what I had done
The records that I made
And now there is a way for me
To have a little trade
My words they are acceptable
To put upon the net
And so I can in time
Remuneration get
But all I need's a start in this
A little trust from others
Those who have the means
To free a little cash
And give me of their stash
But now that I've no means of life
No living wealth at all
I still can say these words

And lift a little smile
When say them to myself I do
A smile comes to my face
So here my dear I give to you
Words so full of grace
They'll light your soul from deep within
They'll lift your eyes to heaven
You too will know the freedom
Etched upon my face
What are these words I hear you say
Please say them now and go
You've wandered far enough today
Shut up and have your say
You have me wondering what you'll say
My soul your hurting too
I know you mean things to be bright
But your leading me astray
Yes, yes my dear I do do that
For that's the play of life
To catch you off your guard and tell you
The simple words to say
Just be kind and gentle to yourself
Don't force it or be false
You simply feel the gentlest touch
Of loving beauty all
They're coming now I hear you say
They're coming from your soul
I see the light within your face

That radiance in your eyes
Just say with me and you'll be free
To soar upon the Earth
And journey over mountain high
And soar in to the sky
Three simple words,
'I love me'

Let's Go Higher

Today I wrote a tangled note
To ascend to higher spaces
A process I've been chasing
Since you were quite young
I know we haven't talked
About this temporal gap
Will there be a problem
I don't think so
At least I hope not
I'm hoping that this will finally
Resolve material matters
So life can begin to flow
Most beautifully
It is what you deserve
It is what I
Hope and sincerely pray for

Closing the Gap

Nearly there
Just a little while
Will I see you, will I smile
I hope so
I'm feeling better now
Although nothing has happened
I know that God will provide something
Even if man can not
Even if they don't see it
Yet I feel it
You're in my soul now
And before you I bow
My lady I adore thee
You are the Queen of the Sidhe
Come to me in this life
A beauteous royal presence
The essence of womanly glory
Now that is a story to be told
Will it be as I've foretold
Will you say yes to me
I know you won't say no
But you might not say anything
I am so uncertain
So unsure
You fill my heart with
Your heavenly light

I can feel your presence now
As the distance closes
Let's take to a bed of roses
And enjoy
Each other for a while
I seem to be quite blatant
My shyness dissolving
I am resolving to
Continue my journey
Whatever it takes

To Teach a Thing or Two

Today I start something I've been waiting
Twenty one years to do
As it's slightly more than that
Since I left on an extraordinary journey
I faced many challenges
I overcame many obstacles
I sweated long hours
Toiling at my computer
I encountered thousands of people
I spoke on television, radio, the pub
All about my passion for knowledge
Purely taught from the heart of life
Taught with a passion for compassion
The type of passion you bring out in me
Overnight I messaged contacts
All over the world
I was contacted by Irish television news
By UCC
I have started to write a paper
Which I will dedicate to you
The queen of my quantum mind
For you are my inspiration
My guide in this world
A world I barely recognise anymore
I want to get you a third present
You will have the other two

As befitting a queen
One to garland your beautiful neck
The other to gaze upon the wall
It is a light house I know well
A beacon which lights the darkness
On a stormy night
Just as you lit my darkness
During the dark days last winter
I thank you for that care
The paper I started yesterday
Is beyond the comprehension
Of most working mathematicians and physicists
Mainly because they are bound in chains
By formal logic
But I have gone beyond that into Alice's kingdom
Which queen are you
Or, I suspect you are a new queen
The white queen of pure beauty and truth
Like me you are an innocent
You are easily hurt
But you are a fighter
You taught me to fight
The meek shall not inherit the Earth
The Warriors of Knowledge shall create
Heaven on Earth
A place where every child will grow
In total knowledge
A place where they will be able to explore

Their universe
Under the compassionate guidance
Of great teachers
Men and women trained by us
Today we begin that
Just in a gentle way
Tell me if I go too fast
You will anyway
You always do
That's what I truly love about you
Your untrammelled honesty
That's it
We begin today

Changing Times

Even though things are shit I don't feel sad
I am not depressed
'I love me,' creeps out of my heart
There is no sorrow in my veins
There is joy at meeting you yesterday
Of spending time
Playing cards
Bantering
You had my letter in your hand
May haps I should write another
From wherever I am, I don't know
Where I shall sleep tonight
I know I'll be fine
But it's time to broadcast the truth
This has begun, the war has begun
I don't like doing that
But in this information game
Words are king

You looked beautiful yesterday
As always your smile captures my heart
I don't think you thought much of my maths
I don't know what to do
I know that all of the psychological shit
Is false
They do not know what they are doing

They cannot measure human intelligence
I know you love your kitten so dearly
For you are the best mum in the world
For you I will fight on
And create a school
For all our children

Smiling Inside

You are beautifully in my head
You occupy a special place in my soul
You cheer my heart when it is sad
The light in your eyes
Dance laughter in to existence
For me you are very special
A real cracker
Not to be trifled with
I purr to myself with the thought
Of you enfolded in my arms
My own cuddly teddy

Winning the War

Today is victory day
Today I initiate and win the war
On ignorance
Ignorance comes in two flavours
Lack of knowledge can be forgiven
Lack of manners is uncouth
You too have faced these challenges
You too have been torn to shreds
By an arrogant system
Which acts not with compassion
They poison the beauty of our lives
With callous barbs
Shards of fragmented knowledge
Information cutting us to the core
Often we are powerless to resist
But I have become powerful
Simply because I have nothing to loose
Except you perhaps
Please give me time
To prove to you that I can provide
A stable place for you
In this crazy world
That is my challenge
Then perhaps you will
Give me your hand

Night Moves

How I would love to spend the night with you
Just to dream away into
The consciousness of Heaven
That is the most important thing
About being together
You enter into a shared experience of sleeping
Of course there are other benefits as well
Ones which make us all smile
One which makes me titter and giggle
How out of this are we going to wriggle
Hopefully with great sensuosity

Decisive Action

Where am I going with all of this
Only time will tell
Despite the obvious difficulty I continue to fight
This is no longer a game of cat and mouse
I don't even have a house
Well I do in a way
But it would rob my life
Of living
What am I to do to resolve
My issues
I truly don't know
Do you, do you have any advice
I know you say I should create a diversion
But diversion assumes that they will engage
What happens when they simply ignore you
Time and again they refuse
To interact
That is the common ploy today
I keep on trying, today
As every day, I have always done
I know it's not fun
But I won't run, away from the role I chose
Something will give
And then hopefully
I will have the ability
To build a life that can

Include you
My Queen, my quantum guide
Now I am sort of despondent
Waiting for something to happen
But it seems that all is gone quiet
I must plan an attack on the hidden enemy
The complacency of ignorance
It is lonely being here on my own
I didn't choose this role
I tried to deny it
It chose me just as much
And now I must act decisively

A Simple Life

I must remember you when I write
Sometimes I write so much it hurts your head
That is never my intention
It's just my invention is so great
Great in quantity not necessarily in brevity
Brevity was never my strong point
For it being the soul of wit
I don't know
With what wit do I do it
I don't sit long enough
I do with you
Sit that is
And enjoy those doey eyes
That twinkle and sparkle with life
Life lived for simple joy
Oh! That my life could be so

Sole Warrior

My mind is not in a great spot at the moment
All seems lost
I have no resources with which to continue
All promises were false
No honour is left in the world
I place great value in honour
I am waiting to hear what you will say
But I have to fight my way
I am prepared to battle ignorance
But ignorance is a coward
Slipping away into dim complacency
In a way I wish I too could subsume
To it's charm
Sure what harm do we do
If we do nothing
I have been at this so long
Battling, that I know
No other life
My father inculcated it in me
My mother too
You too are a fighter
I need your advice
So as not to be so alone

Night Love

My dearest of the quantum night
I met you in the dark
I really do love
Your certainty in an
Uncertain world
You show leadership where others falter
You don't pretend sympathy
Like the crocodile
And gobble up the unsuspecting
No you empathise
With words of truth
Am I right to hope that some day
You and I may go beyond
Friends
And scale the lofty peaks
Of pure love

Chasing Ephemeral Life

I must be careful not to push you away
This always happens with that which we seek
Too much
Our desire reaches out from within
Seeking to grasp the ephemeral
For one such as you
Who flits in and out of my life
The fleeting encounters with you
Are as a summer breeze
Lifting my soul from the cares I have
But you too have your cares
Fleet of foot you guide your life
To your ends
All I hope is that our ends
Can become entangled
In a common bond of friendship and respect
Aiming for the same goals
Respecting our differences
And celebrating our common goals
To achieve our own dreams
And blossom in the full joy
Of shared happiness

Queen of Beauty

I smile when you are not near
My fear has dissolved into truth
The truth and beauty of life is all I see
Oh! What it is to be me
The maddening energy of desire
Now flowing with gentle assuasion
Through my veins
Informed by my heart
You play your part in this
A glory to have you as a friend
The next bend in the road
Will turn the universe
Into a kingdom of pure knowledge
A fitting tribute
For our queen of celestial light
Gentle flowing knowledge from your soul
Precise and exact
Extracting a promise from me
To build what I have set out to do
And present it to thee
To last for eternity

Queen of the Free

Back again under this holy mountain
I pray to thee
I see you in my mind's eye
And I smile
I reflect the beautiful feeling
That you inspire in me
You are my queen
The lady of the night
Who dreamed me into existence
I dream of thee
And you set me free

Pleading to a Queen

I see your face within this place
As you walk along the beach
Picking cockles from the shore
And periwinkles galore
We fill the pot up to the brim
With nature's wonderful bounty
Your smile it lights the fire within
And banishes my sadness
For too long now the years have been
When I've struggled on alone
The searing pain that cripples
Hurting to the bone
But now with you the burden lifts
And shards of happiness
Through sand it shifts
So come to me way down in Kerry
And make me once and ever merry
For I love you, you do know that
I love you all and ever
The pain it mellows in my soul
When thinking about our role
For you and I will go together
Deep into the heart of Heaven
And find a way to sing and pray
To lead others on this way
For we are meant and always were

Together for to be
From first I saw you with your smile
You're the girl for me
'Twas early on I noticed you
The twinkle in your eyes
They lifted my heart from out the cave
And banished my petulant sighs
So dear, oh! Dear, come down to me
Let's start this life a new
Let's be happy in this land
And create a freshened view
For life is short enough my dear
To be lived with daily fear
I know I've felt it all the time
But now a conjured trick I'll mime
I want to love you in the sand
Your beautiful breasts cupped in my hand
And gently stroke your trouble brow
Your cares melt beneath the plough
For your my Eve and I'm your Adam
And nature's children we will be
With loving tenderness by the sea
We'll create this life again
We'll wander round the darkened shore
As God intended us
You'll see that I'm a man of words
With a gift to conjure gold
For gold there is within you dear

A golden heavenly crown
I will present it to you too
When you come down to me
There's sadness in these words I know
But not of pain or loss
No, no, it's just the pining pain
The pain that you're not here
So come to me when you are ready
You'll see what I do see
That Heaven lives upon this Earth
In Cloghane by the sea

Tachyon Queen

I cannot stop writing about you
I won't stop thinking about you
For you light up my heart
A heart that has been lonely
These past decades
Lonely for hope
Lonely for friendship
Lonely for the gentle touch of a lady

A lady such as you
With true passion
A passion for friendliness
A passion to see that all is done right
By our children
You infect me with passion
Support me in your own quirky way
For you are the queen of quirkiness
Come to quinquill a new reality
Into existence
A reality where
The certainty of formal logic
Is replaced by the skill in action
Of mental computation
A place of dynamic movement, so fast
That knowledge is instantly
Relayed around the world

Brains light up at the shared experience
Broadcast
By
Our Tachyon Queen

Sea Queen

More lines do flow from out my head
Lines which capture you
The essence of certain beauty
Perhaps to good to be true
Am I in doubt of how I feel
I hear you silently squeal
I thought he was certain of his love for me
He invited me to the sea
There is no doubt within my mind
No adversity of any kind
Perhaps a little when it comes to settle
How to live with you refined
For as we speak, I'm stone flat broke
I cannot get a penny
Malicious people try to stop
My knowledge flowing out
I know you mean well when you say
To rest my weary mind
But I must go and run a mile
Brush this ignorance in to a pile
For then we'll light it in our fire
That fire of tachyon light
That process faster than the laws
Of George's limiting logic
For I can teach them how to go
Beyond this temporal world

Where they'll find immediate
A connection to my soul
For I'm the soul of computation
The essence of this skill
And with you by my side my dear
We can become an unstoppable will
For we can conquer the whole world
We'll light a fire of knowledge
Just like the one I lit that day
The morning shortest day
When on a slab of rock I was
Festooned with sparkling tweets
The messages I got that day
Did fill my soul with light
And start the journey that I'm on
To rid this world of fear
For fear is not a learned thing
Really it's not there
It will dissolve in time from all
Then in Heaven we'll all fall
Till then we must at once confuse
Purveyor's of rubbish, let's them amuse
With jokes and tales from our great land
They'll know that change is right at hand
For change comes dripping down from Heaven
It drips with golden light
So now you see what I search for
You see what I can do

I love you, will you come to me
So we can see the sea

Snow Queen

A bitter breeze from North North East
Does herald a weather's change
Your mantle decks the lofty peaks
With flecks of frost in range
It is time for summer to be gone
Long lasting bees gone too
They fed upon our gracious thoughts
And left a wonderful view
For they've their queen as well you know
Queen of the summer's day
And she does light upon our soul
And flickering dances play
But whiteness does appear up there
You dust the peaks a new
In truth your beauty does outshine
That wondrous glorious view
So stay up there my love all day
Stay there with greatest grace
Then I can see you any time
And praise this heavenly place

Queen of Light

My heart is lighting again
It seems very variable at the moment
One little thing can send it yawing away
Into outer space
The proper place
For a cosmic heart
A heart full of gold
A golden light suffusing a throbbing
Glowing orb of pure love
That's all for you
Yes I can see you in my arms
We sing a song in unison
We belong together
On this Earth
Or in our own Heaven
The Heaven we will create
Beyond the reach of mortal men
But we will create a stairway
There
Made of pearly glowing metal
Cool to the touch
But warm inside
A stairway sure of step
With unmistakable instructions to traverse
The bounds of this Earth
And transcend normal life

To reach
Utopia

Eternal Queen

You're in my head again, so much that it hurts
I hunger for you
I hunger to touch you
To be with you
To make love with you
To explore your every nook and cranny
To touch you in ways only a true lover can
I feel you in me
I want to be in you
To love you deeply, with my soul
Oh! God it is painful
I never knew how painful love can be
Please set me free
And come to me
Marry me
Be with me
For eternity

When All is Said and Done

I am finished my queen
There is nothing more I can do
Either all my plans work
Or the world sinks into the complacency
Of no compassion for anyone
I thank you for guiding me from afar
And I hope that my dreams with thee
Have an entrance into this reality
For I am as I said, totally in love with you
Even though you remain quiet
As I told you to do
If this doesn't work then, I have
Nothing to offer you
And I could not ask you to join me here
Let us hope that somewhere there is someone
Who can understand
It's all very simple really
My CV only covers half of it
There's still so much in my physiology
That even I don't know what's next
If only I had a few people I could work with
You most of all, you bring the joy out of me
I loose my seriousness
And smile at your smile
I can see you now in my head
And you light up my soul

Let that be my role for thee
I know you'll say wait and see
But I really need you in my reality
As I have said I will do what it takes
I don't know what else I can do
Except may be
Love you
That's it, the book is finished
Were you a dream
Was I dreaming all I wrote
I hope not
Because I still wish to close the circle
And dream with thee
But not from afar
I wish to dream with thee with such
Tender loving care
That they will need a jackhammer to prize us apart
And get some work out of us
Won't that be great
Not having to worry about money
It's all I have to hope for
I have to believe in myself
I wouldn't be here otherwise

Queen of the Night

There is a line which which joins this light of ours
I know you see it although you do not say
We are connected deep within this world
Connected through the soul of life
I give you messages to see
My actions are most honourable to thee
A deluge of information
Transformation for to bring
For you do honour me with thought
That of nought and nothing
For nothing's where I start all this
From out of that our universe flows
It flows along the line of subtle spaces
Fills up to light our human graces
The Janus face does open up the door
To Heaven as we've seen before
I knew I said that this was at an end
But writing does give meaning to my life
So bear with me a while and you will see
The beauty of the mountain and the tree
The tree of life I planted with great care
The fruits of knowledge surely it will bear
I dedicate my life to thee most one and all
To lift this pallid world from out the fall
The fallen garden we observe, that's bare
No nourishment from Heaven, I declare

And let the beauteous souls, all have their say
Yes we can do it now, we're nearly there
My love
We have the plough
That celestial body sure points us to the star
About which our existence does revolve
When this is fully known our life will change
And Earthly beings to Heaven will evolve
For now I must continue on my journey
Guided by you
My dark and lustrous queen

The Fourth Egg

For Patricia

From Letters to my Love

Reflections on making the greatest journey

To be honest with someone is a very perilous thing, at least while they are alive. After they have made the great journey into the unknown, honesty is a precious thing as we try to honour their life and our time with them. I was married with Patricia for nearly twenty five years and whilst not all our life together was enjoyable, we had some great times and like the lives of many couples today we parted too soon. In this collection of poetry written in the months after her death, in 2019, I have tried to work through some of the emotions I felt on that occasion.

Death's Quandary

Maybe, maybe, maybe
We live in a land of make believe
Dreams come and go forever
But life clings to its reality

Death has no bearing
An unwelcome visitor it is not
Untimely maybe so
But a natural part of living

So fear not to ask us questions
Do not be afraid of being uncertain
Ascertain the truth of life
By searching in your heart

For she still lives within us
Even though in a different form
She lives and laughs and smiles
At the quandary she has created

Seeking Signs

Slivers of light live in the night
As you cast a shadow in the midday sun
Your passing had drained the energy from my soul
But now it is coming back
Full to the brim with unexpected plentitude

A realisation that your life is not over
Has become paramount to me
For you are too beautiful a person to be wasted
On a single existence
For God in his infinite wisdom wishes to see
    the persistence of beauty

So dearest love wake up to my yearning for a sign
A template of a message as my father gave to me
When I learned to transcend
Pass through the veil of silence
And shout through our corner of the universe

God's Plan

To lose you at such a young age
Was an affront
An affront to the certainty of life
An affront to all that is good
It creates a feeling of uncertainty
In the yearned for

We all seek to live within
Well defined patterns
To know what today or tomorrow
Brings
But your death shows
That God's plan is greater
Than our meagre grasp of it

Unrequited Love

My darling now that you are gone
My yearnings for you will never be assuaged
Now physical and mental yearnings
Will have to be replaced by spiritual ones

For you have become a spiritual being
A wisp of the wind, a lap of the water
You have entered the totality of creation
A beautiful component to universal being

But it does not stop me hoping and craving for you
Wishing that I could hear your voice again
I hear it in my spiritual being
But I know that will grow fainter

So love of my life hear this
Whatever corner of creation you have gone to
I too will join you in time
And we can do crosswords again

Crosswords

Your tongue peeks from your mouth
As you focus attention on a daily ritual
That is what I missed most
As we separated and divorced

Perhaps if I paid you more attention
And took my head from lofty heights
We could have stayed the course
And loved until eternity

I brought hell on earth to your door
When I simply couldn't take it any more
The four horseman clamoured in my head
And filled our house with dread

But you persisted and won out in the end
Your sense of survival put me on the mend
It took time, patience and separation
But the cross words ceased and were replaced
With respect

This took time and effort on both our parts
A silence of the chattering in our relationship
But thank you my love for being strong enough
And saving both our lives

Shoptalk

Inevitably our conversation would turn to education
You didn't like me questioning the system
You felt threatened by it
But I was a questioner at heart
I too had to play my part
And discover a way to tell the truth
Without destroying normality

Such are the ways of progress
The current state must linger
Move through from future to present to past
Then evolution is balanced
And progress is based on superfluid flow

My dear we often said
That if these walls had ears
Our kitchen would be
The most educated edifice on Earth

Shadowlands

I walked there thinking of you
Crossed over the boundary from living to dead
But this is a place never to be visited
Again

Three times I sought release from the pain of living
But each time something drew me back
Now I realise my duty is to be a father
And maybe even a grandfather

The shadowlands are best left unexplored
Occupied by ghosts of the living
Troubled souls sensitive to misfortune
A crisis lived life in daily suffering

Now it is time to effect a positive attitude
Not to let temporary despair become
overwhelming
Open up our heart
To the creative force of the universe
And banish shadows to the nether regions

Keep Smiling

We trawled through your boxes of photographs
And in every one you beamed out your joy
Oh! Precious lady why did I not always see that
I suppose life becomes mundane
If you let it

Looking at those photographs reminded me
Of the great times we shared
We really did enjoy life to the full

Wherever you are I'm sure that you are beaming
Perhaps a new star has just winked into existence
If so we will seek it out and know it by its
brightness

You taught all of us to follow your lead
And celebrate our lives in a perfect way
Curve our lips upward and let the bliss flow

For you are a blissful being
Knowing now the true meaning of happy
molecules
Unfortunately you had to leave us
For me to fully appreciate your worth

But I know that you are in my heart
And all that is required

Is for me to turn my attention gently within
And I hear you whispering 'hon'

Favourite Place

The cauldron sits in a quite glen
A few miles from *Carraigh an Droichead*
A place I visited more than once

One time in midwinter
With snow deep on the ground
I stopped in a pub
Before launching into song
Singing my own song
I left a dubious gathering
And wandered in the snow

Again I returned another midwinter's night
A night of three alignments
To launch my book of verse
In an old druidic place
A place where druids once gathered
Three of us recreated their song
Accompanied by a shaman's drumbeat

Once on a summer's evening
I decided to bathe in the crystal waterfall
Looking up I saw an astonished professor
Looking down and into the past
He saw a druid step out of history
Unashamedly naked enjoying the waters
Of a favourite place

Too Soon

You were taken from us before
The cock crew in the morning
The day had just begun
When you were struck down
In an instant

My beloved
Your life was just beginning again
After the loss of your best friend
Your travelling partner
To many a far field

The train of joy had barely left the station
With you a passenger on it
When the whistle sounded
And death visited your carriage
The whistle replaced by the tolling funerary bell

Later in time would have been preferable
But we must live with the knowledge
That you were living life to the full
You had fulfilled life's journey
And strolled to the other side of the universe

A Listening Job

You spend your days listening to others
A pious vocation in these impious times
Litanies of pain and suffering
Are laid bare in your parlour
How do you endure
What is your secret
Tell me please for I need your steadiness
I need to be ready for a new life
A new beginning without a wife
For she is dead now
And I am in dread now
I fear the future without her wistful smile
Visiting me once in every short while
Will talking with you make me see reason
And gain succour to survive another season
Please lend me your ear
So that I may listen to my own heart
Listen to the love that flows
Sundering today's reality
To create a new loving future
With my very own self
Renewed and forgiven

For my therapist

Encircling Ireland

Some years ago I returned to Allihies
For the first time since our disaster
It was so pleasant a journey and again
I camped on the beach
Fished and caught a bass
Met the locals in a pub
Was invited home for grub
They noticed me because even then
I was writing poetry
This was during my circumnavigation
Of our holy island

Later I climbed our highest mountain
With our only son
A group of us climbed up the grey place
To the summit adorned with a cross
While on the top I recited my version of
Dán Amerigáin
Reputed to be Ireland's first poem
And Con our guide told the story
Of the invasion of the Milesians

The journey petered out in Galway
As I camped in Eyre Square and
Participated in an occupation
Of that wonderful place

What genuine people I met
Young people who wanted
To make a difference in a considered way

It had started in
The occupation of Cork
With the clap of cymbals
A buddhist prayer
And a rendition of
Ciúin le Miúin

What a wonderful island we live on
Wonderful places
Wonderful people
Let us not forget that
As we rush headlong into the future

Non-Jury Trial

You were always so proud of the fact
That you could never serve on a jury
You had not become corrupted by life
And you could not bring this corruption
Into your work

I was called for jury service once
Empanelled for a week in the court room
I never had to serve on an individual case
So I too did not have to face the corruption
And let it seep into my life

Not that there is anything wrong
With the judicial system
It's just that
It is outdated as a means of preventing crime
Far better to use consciousness based methods
Then see the demolition of every courthouse
On Earth
And the eradication of criminality in all its forms

Then we can really see a bright future
A future full of bliss
That simple essence so dear to every human heart

Warm Friends

We walk about looking down at the cobbles
Eyes averted to escape the penetrating gaze
Ashamed at our insecurity
We lapse into moments of solitude

Look up I say to you and enjoy the day
For tomorrows night may never come
And life's too short to be glum
Resist depression

For she was never once depressed in her life
Never knew a day without joy
Lived life in blissful ignorance
Of suffering

Not that life did not throw it share of burdens
Loads she bore with patience and forbearance
She shared some with friends
And as such lived a better life than most

So now that her time has past
She will remain exemplar to all
Of a life lived simply
Supporting and supported by friends

A Conversation

So now my talking goes nowhere
You have no means to respond
At least not in the physical realm
The response must be more subtle
Inner knowledge expressing itself
Through intuition
The language of the soul

Luckily I am well practiced in such
Nearly thirty years transcending
Gives me a feel for the subtle reality
But still my attention wanders
The language of the soul is so gentle
That it easily remains unheard

So talk to me my darling
Whisper sweet nothings to my heart
Nourish me with your love
For I need your support
In this time of sorrow

Then we can begin a proper dialogue
Whispering to each other
The truths of eternity

The Poetics Of Language

Language structures the brain
And in turn is formed by the brain
Words are formed by the brain physiology
From faint impulses in consciousness
This is a self referral process
And relies on the innate structure of the universe

Every brain is capable of tapping into this
    cosmic process
Is capable of becoming truly self referral
Once it is trained to transcend the daily reality
And enter the field of pure unbounded intelligence
The fundamental reality which underlies totality

Then the brain physiology becomes invincible
Every thought, word and deed
Is supported by the myriad laws and tendencies in
    nature
And every action expresses the poetics of language
In a kingly fashion

Opening Up

It was funny to sit on the chair again
Glass of water in hand
And relay the sad tale of your death
To a man of compassion

He allowed me time to sniffle a bit
As I related your sad demise
I felt so special as I sat on the chair
Another being paying close attention

The tears ebbed and flowed
Not great waves
Just like the tide on a pebbled beach
A subtle susurration in the background

He shared his own story of the death of his parents
Illustrated the stages of grief from experience
He is such a gentle soul
That I too shed a tear

So now the process has begun
I need have no more trepidation
Tears may fall or not, my heart may open or close
To accept solace from wherever it comes

Struggling Through

My mind is addled with fear
No thoughts come from within
Yet words flow onto the page
With practised skill

The energy of writing
Flows with perfection
When you listen to your soul
All makes sense

Life is a battlefield
Caught between opposing forces
Creative energy flourishes
By reference to itself

Curving back in to my own self
I pick up the essence of creation
And produce wonder lines
Even in the face of adversity

Confusion Reigns Supreme

You are dead and my heart breaks
Normal service is suspended
As we try to come to terms with
Your passing

Oh! My dear where do we put our trust
When one so young as you can be taken
Taken in the prime of your life
Taken to the bosom of a selfish God

First there was denial that this was happening
We sought to run away from the truth
Then our minds were sent into a spin
As we viewed the grim reality

I tried to initiate a rosary
But my mouth was unable to form
The well known words
Others continued on and fought through the
    confusion

Now at one removed, that is a distant time
And confusion has been replaced with a
Dull acceptance
You are dead now so get on with it

Light A Penny Candle

It doesn't take much to go to a Church
Search in a pocket for loose change
And perform an act of remembrance
Light from another
A little flame of love

For such is your existence now
Nourished by love
And simple acts of kindness
You exist as a flame on a pedestal
A flame among many others who have passed

This is one thing I can do to keep the contact
Light a flame every day
And give you the chance
To come and have your say
Inscribing light with your love

For you exist in the light now
The light of God's love
Surrounds you
My dear I miss you
I don't know where I am

A Mother's Love

No one knows the depth of their passion
The absolute power they posses
To protect
To nourish
To love
Their progeny

For they will go beyond any rational thought
If anyone seeks to harm in any way
Their beloved child
Their most beloved offspring
The product of their inner being

For motherhood must be one of
God's greatest gifts
A real challenge in this day and age
Balancing everything to maintain stability
In a hectic life

I'm glad to have met you both
My wife
My mother
Two special ladies in my life

Warrior Lady

You shoot through the stars
On a mighty steed composed of cosmic dust
For you have become a celestial being
You have transcended normal reality
To assume your rightful place
In the universe

Many mourned your passing
Many tears were shed
Gracious people paid their respects
To you, in response to your deep
And caring nature

I know this, as I spent many years with you
You defended your being with tenacity
And fought to maintain dignity against all odds
My dearest, dearest, love
If only you were here again
Perhaps everything could have been different

Simple Sums

We sat around the kitchen table and planned
Plotting the next phase of education
Pete, Jim and myself
Dedicated to knowledge

Our efforts were fruitful in that
We exposed the potential
For a new approach to mental computation
An approach known then as Simple Sums

For mathematics is not all logic
Logic forms a very small part of it
Mostly it is skill in applying
Simple rules mirroring the actions of the brain

You brought it in to your school
And proved the benefit to shyer students
They enjoyed knowing non-standard techniques
Ways to brighten the brain

We made a presentation to departmental inspectors
And they suggested a computerised approach
Thus the animation techniques were developed
And animathics was born

Not enough support in the end
For so subtle an idea

But the next generation can run with it
And create math with smiles

Mountain Glory

The peloton had reached the Pyrenees
When I was called from the television
To assist in the delivery of our baby
So tiny, and yet, you were so tiny
You bore your pregnancy with joy
For a few days you were on cloud nine
It was as if you were on a high
Your doctor met you on the corridor
And said you should be resting
You smiled and said you had to visit
Your sister in law
Unfortunately the glory did not last
As your father died
But you bore it with great dignity
The true spirit of a mountaineer
Rising to the challenges of life
With all conquering energy
Now, thirty years later
We concelebrate those times
When we remember you
At your most courageous

Citronella

Your favourite fragrance
The bugs always seemed
To target your fair skin
A skin I cherished for its silky smoothness

How I loved your touch
You had the most delicate hands
Delicate in size and shape
Delicate in actions
As you caressed me
To my very soul

Now this is just a memory
But one so precious
That I will cherish it
To eternity

Inner Music

We communicate in so many levels
Saying sweet things to each other
But the tone of voice is so important
Soft, mellow and strong

I heard a voice yesterday
A voice I had forgotten
Cultured tones from the depth of being
He comforted me in my grief

Now I must remember your tone
For that is all I have to hear
The music of your being
The essence of your existence

For Stewart

Before Your Time

Why were you taken so young
You had not the pleasure of growing old
You had not become a grandmother
A task you would have cherished

At least you were a grandaunt
And what a lady you must have been
I know what that feels like
As I have met my grandees

You were barely retired
With myriad plans for the future
They all involved art in some form
Your secret pleasure

You made up for the fact
That art was not your primary degree
Too young you said to go to college
But now surpassing most

The time for recognition has come
When your art will hang together
And people will truly realise
That you were an artist of our time

Take It Easy

The task at hand now is to cherish your memory
Not to be selfish in my writing
To allow you due and careful consideration
It is so easy for me to dominate your memory
And all this becomes about my own ego
I will try my best to cherish you
As you would have wanted
With dignity and restraint

A Song Of Loss

The symphony of song sings for thee
A chorus of angels lights up our heart
For you are newly joined to the celestial throng
Newly enthroned in the kingdom of Heaven

My dear look down on us when you get a chance
Those of us who have been left askance
Knocked out of our comfortable lives
Asking questions for which no answers come

Tears will not wash away the loss
Anger does no good at all
Words sculpted in a heartfelt way
Seem to have a comfortable say

For you are missed dearly
There is no cheerful memory
Which can compensate us
For your death

Heed Advice

Open your ears to the advice of others
Do not live in a solitary bubble
For others can see the pain
Etched on your face
Otherwise you may face a great challenge
Greater even than my death
Listen to me my love
And take care of your health
For you are now my factor
In our boy's life
He needs you now more than ever
Although he may not say it
For he is a man now
And will not always show his face
So fair thee well my love
Heal well and run tall
Look out for yourself
Then life will be a ball

Foot Sore

A week to ten days had passed as I wore bad shoes
Normally they would be ok
But these were not normal times
It slipped from my mind the advice
We had been given
To wear appropriate shoes at all times
Mine caused a blister on the sole of my foot
Which I ignored
Until two nights ago when my foot swelled
Then I began to realise the seriousness
Of the situation
But now my foot is bound professionally
And I'm on antibiotics
These will help to heal the soul
Of a weary traveller

Heartstrong

Thank you for your wilfulness my love
You warned me of the seriousness
Of my situation
Comparing it to your death
This time I could not ignore you
As I ignored you many times before

Oh! What a patient lady you were
And me ignorant of your pain
You never once spoke harsh words
In the face of my ignorance

So let me now say sorry my love
For any crass and stupid things
I may have done
For I was just acting out
The uncertainty of abuse

Abuse knows no end
And continues for a lifetime
Hurting those closest
To a cherishing heart

Now that you are gone my love
There is little I can say
Or do

Except shed a tear
For a wondrous heart

Bereft Of Fun

Normally at this time of day
I would scan the TV listings
To see if there was anything on
But now I find them most uninteresting
Television life seems so unreal
In the face of this new reality

Are you gone to a place
With such communication
Or does mental telepathy rule
So many questions I yearn for
Answers not forthcoming
From God's paradise

Does this poetry come from you
Do you inform my intuition
These words are formed in my heart
A heart filled now with sorrow
Not a crushing sorrow
But sweet and exquisite to your loss

I know another day will come
When your loss dims
And I can shine a light on joy
And have fun again
But for the moment
I lie quietly bye

Beaming Words

The words flow out of nowhere
From uncreated to created
Expressed through a living vessel
God's message is heralded
For we are all a product of his grace
Simple words occupying a place
In time they express great emotion
Sorrow enfolds itself within a notion
This cannot be happening we say to you
She is gone and there is nothing to do
What will these words accomplish
At the end of time
Rise up now my dear for it is true
Let me help you express your joy
The end of days are nigh
We can relax with a sigh
It is all a dream
She'll walk through the door with a beam

Forgive Me My Love

Now that you are gone from us
You know the full picture
You have entered the state of all knowingness
You have transcended time, past, present and future
And are become one with God
The supreme cosmic intelligence which rules
    the universe
You have added a sweet note of compassion
To God's realm

So listen to me my love
Listen to my heartfelt pleading
Forgive my crass and stupid behaviour
Behaviour I know which hurt you
And drove you to action
Action which caused you to separate
From your one true love

But we became friends again
You respected my reconciliation with life
I became as you remembered me
A kind sensitive human being

Blocked Words

Oh! My dear the words are reluctant to flow
There is a blockage in the creative process
My mind is all askew at your loss

I can feel the thoughts flowing within
But the pain in my heart seizes
The exuberance of expression

Dear God, my mind gasps
How could you have taken her
And she with a long life to lead

Now it is up to me to fulfil
Life's dream
My love, you would never forgive me
For wallowing in despair

The Loss Of Love

My love you have left this Earth pining
For another glimpse of you
Just a beam of your smile
Would be enough
But your time was through
You had completed in your shortened life
A myriad of things
Made many friends and succoured too
So now that you are gone
We shall have to persist without you
And get on with
Remembering and honouring your life

A Reluctant Ear

You always heard them first
As I recited day after day
A litany of words
Expressed from deep within

I had no other audience
So you were elected
A willing or unwilling accomplice
To my versification

Then one night a brainwave struck
Go to the nearest radio and recite
There I met Zeke
Who relieved you of your duty

Other places followed as I gained confidence
That yes I had something to say
And there were people willing to listen
Are you listening now

A Scottish Journey

We crossed by ferry to Stranraer
Unsure of travelling through
A fractured part of our country
Where we found a yellow stained pub

With a ladies room fit for a queen
You were crowned
And had become
My queen of compassion

Next day we crossed the Clyde
Ten miles short of Glasgow
And took the Oban road
Destined for a familiar place

From Oban we crossed to Mull
And wondered at the long horned cattle
A village with the name of Tralee
Reminded me of home

We saw a kidnapped place
A golden eagle in the sky
The holy island of Irish saints
And many scampi shops

Then we moved on to Skye
Felt immediately at home

Listening to a familiar Irish band
Playing gently from a stand

Stein it was we were in
And we marvelled at
The cliffs abruptly falling
Into a quiet sea

Then back to Edinburgh we went
Found lodgings cheap to rent
Were blessed in those festival days
With a room under the castle

There is more of this story to tell
And it will keep for another day
The honey month we spent in Scotland
To start our life of play

A Spiritual Gem

I went down to West Cork to write
And came back with a gemstone
A little piece of knowledge
Bestowed upon me by Mair

For my mind was crushed
With academic pursuits
Seven long years
Of a strained mental race

Gradually my mind relaxed
As I polished the precious stone
Twice a day
Polished it until it sheened
Throughout my soul

Now decades later
I reap the reward
As I mourn for you
But not overwhelmed

Nature's Love

Looking into the past I see you smiling
Always with a beaming aspect on your face
Never a dull frown
Oh! Where did we go wrong

For our love was due to last
From now until eternity
Invincible in the face of life
Never missing a heartbeat

But we changed with life's changing seasons
Inevitably entropy took hold
Like a dull beat in the morning
Sounding its destructive knell

For nature's forces are powerful
Whether physical, mental or spiritual
And a stone cast in the morning
Ripples its effects till evening

So watch out all who care
Danger lurks everywhere
Be vigilant in the face of life
Then you'll remain husband and wife

A Common Passing

Just one of many that happened that day
You passing has affected us in many a way
You took fright with our heart
Breaking pieces into every little part
Oh! My dear where are you gone
Is there nothing we could have done
To alleviate your pain
And helped you to gain
Sustenance enough to stay
We had another game to play
Now it is just another story
To tell how you entered glory
And walked the stairway of light
With nary another fight
How common a sight it was
To lose you to death

Christmas Lights

Under the darkling sky we saw
Three lights at Christmas
Out the back porch
Of Nana's house

The lowest light was white
Higher than that was red
And then highest of all
Out of this Earth was starlight

Three kings you said will come tonight
Our baby is safe in the manger
Tucked within the bosom of my family
In the house in Bothernasup

Taking A Long View

This is a much more complex process
Than I had anticipated
The task of coming to terms with your death
Handling your personal emotional legacy
In a way that is both honest and fair
For I must be fair to both of us
We were not a perfect couple
We had our problems
From an early stage
So I must take precautions
To seek the truth
Please help me to
There is no other way forward

Conflicting Tendencies

When the rosy glow of first love faded
The truth of our situation blossomed
We were from opposite tribes
Used to different rules

Your's were bound to a tradition of meals
Mine to rambling wheels
I sought to bring my tradition with me
Whenever we were under your family tree

But you were uncompromisingly stubborn
We must be back for dinner or else
We would upset
Long held family traditions

Unbending rules honed over decades
Every family has them
You never complained in my domain
At least I never heard you

An Emotional Edifice

My whole physiology expresses a thought
Feels an emotion at its most refined
Then brings it into awareness
Where it is made conscious to my mind

At present my body is pining
Feeling guilty at your loss
Resisting the urge to open up
And speak plainly

When a word is mistaken
Assumed to be one way rather than another
Then I too will be adjudged
A criminal in an emotional trial

These no doubt are complex issues
To intricate for me to process consciously
Better leave it to my subtle self
Much more in touch with truth and beauty

For these are what I hope for
To pick up the most refined feelings
And expressed them with sculpted words
Shaped with care and diligence

Scattered To The Wind

I had a vision of the place I will scatter
The ashes of these letters
A symbolic place to me
As I celebrated a midwinter's dawn
The last year we were together
I flurried on a bus to catch the rising sun
As it rose over South Kerry
Across a glistening sea

I stood on a high cliff
And hurriedly lit a fire
A symbol of the knowledge
Burning in my soul

This point, the furthest west in Ireland
Is steeped in magic, mystery and tradition
A fitting place to light a fire of knowledge
Designed to banish the night

For this will be my offering
To you my dearest love
Before these letters take their wings
And flit about on changing winds

Sunday Dinner Service

We used to enjoy going out on a Sunday
A service of roast beef with all the trimmings
Over looking the sea at Bunnyconellans

Many times we went there
With Michael and Liz
Friends from academia

Then a little bundle of joy arrived
You nourished him in Myrtleville
Watching a match which Mayo didn't win

Later he tried our patience
As we sought to share dinner
On a Mothering Sunday

He was just expressing the natural
Tendencies of a young child
Hemmed in by a wall of adult conversation

Now he himself goes back there
To enjoy a Sunday roast
The next generation following suit

For Eoghan

An Island Dance

We didn't know what to expect
In our national theatre
A group made up of locals
Well practiced many years
They told an island story
At the edge of our awareness
Next parish is America
To where many islanders fled
A harsh life it must have been
Told skilfully in song and dance
Stories of simple pleasures
Stories of sorrowful gales
For children they did die there
When no doctor came
And all who lived have now gone
To a better abode
There are stirrings now as fresh blood
Occupy houses anew
And for at least a six month time
Voices echo with song and rhyme

For Siamsa Tíre

Empty Hours

When you left us we searched for you
Looking into the past we remembered
The bright spirit you once were

You occupy our daily thoughts
Not constantly, but enough
To light a vast stadium

Now that I'm on my own
I must divert my nagging attention
Or else your screaming beaming reality
Will drown me in sorrow

How long will this last
Can anyone tell
How long until I heal
And ne'er hear death's knell

Early Morning Blues

I get up early to write you a letter
Expressing feelings to make me better
But nothing will lift my spirit
Out of a dull feeling of loneliness

Alone I plough this furrow
Feeling frustrated at my lack
Of any type of inspiration
Words created with perspiration

Dear God! Let this nightmare end
Propel me to heaven
Let me talk honestly with you
To lift the blue mood this morning

Searching For You

I peer into the nether regions of my soul
Seeking a spark of light
Seeking your image
Seeking to speak with you

But no light comes forth from the darkness
Your image is bereft of form
And your voice shimmers in silence

My dearest love you are gone from us
We who persist in the land of the living
Wake up to our yearning for thee
And fulfil our dearest wish

Confusion Reigns

I am living in a kingdom of trouble
All about me problems bubble
It is my own personal attitude
That casts a shadow over life

I feel sorry for myself, but no regret
Can make up for your loss
You have gone to a far better place
Filled up with members of the human race

Please dear love help me shoulder this burden
Bestow upon me some rays of light
Lift from my heart the feelings of night
Let me reap the reward of having known thee

My head spins with a constant longing
My heart seeks your belonging
For you brought calm to our centre
Bubbling bliss you allowed to enter

Now after all this trouble and strife
Feeling low at the loss of a wife
A glimmer of hope will shine within
Resolving now and forever to win

Thunder Mountain

Let's go for a walk I said
And see our highest mountain
As we rested in the pool one morning
In the holiday village at Fossa

You weren't the greatest swimmer
And paddled in the pool
Barely trusting me to hold your hand
As your head dipped in the water

Later you got a dose of further immersion
In a mountain stream
Slipping off a rock with boot and sock
It wasn't funny you said as we both laughed

That was a day of torrential rain
Claps of thunder resounding
About Hag's Glen and lakes therein
A day of thunder in Omagh

Stilted Words

This writing is slow and reluctant in coming
Where once words dripped with meaning
They are now shocked into being
Emerging from the essence of solitude
With guarded aspects

Only in verse does freedom roam
Free verse so as not to be burdened
With counting syllables on a rope
Or finding rhyme
Or suitable mime

Now my efforts are not great
The river of emotion is in full spate
But yet I pick up the odd thought
From the market place yet to be bought

Now it ends

A Passion Of Words

I listen to my heartbeat looking for inspiration
The welling words sing within my awareness
Now I can select with judicious care
Nouns and verbs, emotions laid bare

Oh! How do I manage to convey
The feelings I am bound to obey
My powers of discernment are sullied
Emotionally fraught with laboured pains

Now that your passing is almost normal
The depth of pain has eased
The drip drip of tears has ceased
And words flow with exquisite bliss

It is becoming easier
To listen to the language of my soul
And hear a heartbeat's murmur in the morning
Flowing to overflowing with conscious care

So for now I look within with joy
Remembering once we were girl and boy
Life was new to us, a toy
And our passion didn't make us coy

Now so much older in age
Consumed by the world like onion and sage

Words still drip with meaning
And passion is but a memory

An Emblem Of Birth

You smiled when I gave you the golden leaf
Not a four leafed clover of Irish design
But three as in the emblem of Canada
Why this I do not know
But it was bought in a rush
Together with various other
Accoutrements
For a new baby
You gave me a list and I was
A little embarrassed
But the lady smiled at me and knew
A new arrival was heralded
The maple leaf is thirty years old now
Just like our son
One hasn't changed the other has grown tall
From a tissue box, to a six footer
One you were most proud of
The other you wore with pride
Until you died

Stranger My Love

The marriage space
Is a funny place
Occupied by two people
Closer together than evermore
Lumps, bumps and every sore
We were a couple in wedded bliss
With chances of joy I'd never miss
So now your gone, I realise
That you I didn't know
You were a stranger to me
Even on your death

Hidden Places

I met him in a hostel in Baltimore
Top of the hill up from the shore
A tall man by name of Torsten
Running things with German efficiency

I stayed for a week
Glad of shelter I needn't seek
The weather was bad, snow on the ground
After twenty five miles, roads I did pound

One night he approached me in the pub
Wondering where I was going next
Nowhere planned I said to him
I've an idea he responded

So next day we climbed aboard his jeep
And headed to the mountains deep
Near to where there lived a man
Considered a guru in his head

He took me in and gave me a bed
In little more than a summer shed
I paid for it by taking down
A poly tunnel red with rust

Three weeks I stayed there
With a daily grind

Morning chanting in a church
Self proclaimed a holy man

It was a strange experience to me
Deep in the Gaeltacht of West Cork
A Dutch man living a vedic life
Hiding away from all the strife

Eventually I left his place
And took again another space
In fortune's house in Skibbereen
I found a place to vent my spleen

Long Winter's March

It started in a pub in Clonakilty
Where I had gone in
For a pint of lonely comfort
For the first time I was on my own
After twenty five years together
A voice caught my attention
'Why don't you join us?' she said
A young girl by my reckoning
I stayed put for a while then realised
This was just what I needed
A bit of company to jolt me
We had a great night and I was offered
A couch rather than a cold beachside plot
In the morning I headed on my way
And walked throughout a winter's day
My purse was empty and I had no food
But walk I did, I was in the mood
For ten hours or more I carried my pack
And sought a place to lay my sack
Then just before Skibbereen's bright light
I spotted a place to spend the night
The ground was frozen with the snow
A tin of beans made my stomach glow
'Till morning and I had a blast
A full Irish twice did break my fast
The march was finished

And I was glad
My heart was nourished
And I wasn't sad

The Loss Of Innocence

There are many stories told of the effect
Abuse has upon a child
As their warped identity grows
Into adulthood

In my case the greatest of all
Was that loss forever of the
Innocence endowed by personal touch

You restored it with great sensitivity
And I thank you for this my love
From every fibre of my being

Memories Of Love

I sat again and talked of you
The effect you had on my life
A shy sensitive person you were
All except one night
When dangerous liaisons inspired you
To really love me
Oh! How precious that was
A single night of wanton abandon
My dearest I love you for it
Please bring these memories back to me
So that I can hang them on a tree

The End Of Loss

Your loss is a blunt forced trauma
To my psychic body
My spiritual being yearns for truth
Are you happy
Are you sad
Are you alone
Are you, are you, are you, ...
So many questions
No answers
Dear God will it ever end

A Simple Life

Living with you was very special
You had such a simple view
No great thoughts on anything
Just get on with the process in hand
How do you live now
Is it similar

Cloud Dancer

You had such dainty feet
My sister still comments on them
Barely fitting in to children shoes
Was how she remembers

How they could support you
I never knew
Especially when you had the operation
In preparation for our wedding

Oh! My dear how could you
Go through such pain for me
You really were remarkable
A liberating soul and free

Free of the travails of life
You inspired all who met you
Now with your passing day
You dance in the clouds

Getting Bye

How quickly life moves on
We all adhere to living
With great tenacity
Death is no stranger to us
Visiting us through your auspices
It is getting easier to talk about it
No welling tears
No sorrowful feelings
But a simple sense of loss
My darling
We all miss you
But are glad you didn't linger
For such a life
You would not
Have wanted

Cosmic Influence

For some reason I feel deflated
The interview went well
But I'm not elated
Perhaps I will move there
Perhaps I will not
It's all in the hands of the gods now

But you have an influence in this
Greater ever than mine
Let us hope that your influence
Succeeds where mine fails
For you are become powerful
Enough to move the universe

When you speak the universe shudders
You command the voice of God
You compassion influences all things
Truth and beauty are your middle names

So now assume your confident stride
Walk tall among the angels
Whisper great things in the ear
Of those who decide

Imperfection

Now that I have admitted my past
I feel somewhat better
We all have things we would like
To keep hidden
We all have lapses of memory
That in the moment
We regret
Now that I have come forth to you
Will you support me in forgetting
Erasing the official memory
If there is one
And letting your light shine on my soul

Forgive Me A Sinner

Dear Lord, forgive me a sinner
I did not mean to do these things
Throughout my life
I did not mean to transgress
And create havoc
I did not mean to tell
A small lie
A sin of omission
Please Lord, forgive me a sinner

For I am an imperfect soul
I wend my way through life
As best I can
My whole being was sinned against
Whilst very young
And I carry those scars upon me
So please Lord, forgive me a sinner

A Culpable Life

Let us not regret the breaking of the day
Let us live without the sorrow
Beating our breast is not the way
To alleviate the pain of life

For Heaven knows we all make mistakes
No one has the ideal formula
To live a life free of blame
And thereby have perfection on our plate

So my dear what secrets did you harbour
Was there anything you regretted in life
Or were you as you seemed
A blameless person in perfection

University Of Compassion

I entered the room as a shadow
Not knowing what to expect
Who are these people
That I had become one of

Tom cocked an eye
From under his cap
I didn't know him then
But he became a good friend

We travelled together
Like Indian scouts
Him to the front, big chief
Me behind, little man

Gradually their magic worked
As I came back from the brink
Of suicidal thoughts
And seemed happy for a while

After three months I left the room
Convinced that I had graduated
But other trials happened
And I was never redeemed

Today I travel my own road
Seeking counsel with friends or others

Always aware that should I need it
There is a room for me there

Scribble Scrabble

Early in the morning I search for words
Drag them up from the depths of memory
Nice words if I can find them
Honest words at least

Oftentimes I shirk from expressing
The truth as I see it
To honour your memory is my goal
Not to go raking and raking

Please my dear let me find a way
To represent our lives together
To let you have a say
So that our beautiful life may shine

Burning Brightly In The Night

There is a place in my heart that is owned by you
A special place that few have ever seen
For you were known to be joyous beyond repair
Never a dull mood did cross your awareness
How could I have been so foolish
To take you for granted

My dearest, dearest love I know now
What a special person you were
What a place you occupied on Earth
To aid, comfort and listen to others
Always ready to laugh or cry
To help a friend

To me you were like a lustrous flame
Burning brightly in the night
And me a lowly moth

Burned I did become
By your fierce temperament
Your resolute adherence
To what you saw as right
Never to be turned
From your own perfection

A Longing Heart

There is a longing in my heart today
A deep resounding victory over death
For you are passed on to somewhere new
A deep deep colour of cerulean hue

My dear, my love, I can hear you still
Within my heart your voice resounds
You inform my waking moments
And nighttime fetters are unwoken

For now I seek you in the day
When quiet times they are upon me
I dream of thee in every way
And listen to my soul chattering

It is not easy to let you go
Even though we lived apart
My heart yearned to be near thee
Now that will never be

So rest me dear by God you earned it
Sing with the angels clear
I will remember you for all my life
My dear and loving departed wife

An Angelic Being

Where does the time go
When you are young it seems that there is plenty
But as the years accumulate it grows more precious
There is only so much in the land of the living
But for those who have passed there seems an
    eternity
So my dear you have entered the road of truth
For you, there can no longer be any uncertainty
You commune with the angels
And are consumed with joy

Universal Journey

We have become so busy
With barely time to think and talk
Flitting about the world
Predetermined routes to walk

We live in such a changed world
All the boundaries are coming down
Where once stood nation states
They are now lead only by a clown

But deeper forces are at work
Powers totally in tune with nature
They will construct a Heavenly abode
Within the confines of our Earth

Perhaps then you will come back
Of this I can't be sure
You are on your own journey
Through the universe on tour

Keeping Things Private

Secrets are not the same as privacy
The former is a strict thing
The latter one of decency
When we wish to explore a relationship
We do so with a delicate memory
Especially if one party is deceased
For they no longer have a voice
In this realm of ours
We must be gentle
To give them a choice
So now my mind is made up
A private thought is king
With this you can gently sing

Dawn Yawn

Oh! Dear God why can't I sleep
My attention keeps popping
In and out of consciousness
Even though I am sleepy
A state of restful alertness
Eludes me
Even now I am yawning
As I desperately seek succour
Before the dawning

Writing Thoughts Of Love

I arise early in the morning to inscribe my heart
On the pages of my diary of love
With all the truth I can muster
I transform vague feelings of emotion
Into pure thoughts of you

You were such a beautiful creature
Bubbling with effervescent life
Even in the face of great adversity
You never lost your poise
Never once did you despair

Oh! Dearest love
Rest well in your new abode
I am so lucky to have known you
You brightened the lives of so many
And all who knew you shed a tear

The Long Road To Nowhere

Life is a wandering journey
Through an uncertain valley
With a river running through it
A wild river full of whirlpools
A calm river with meadows passing by
A beautiful river soothing to the soul

The river leads from source to sea
Wanders along from birth till death
Just like life passing through
Never knowing what to expect
Never knowing what's around the corner
Never knowing when bliss will come

We do not fully appreciate life
Except when it is over
So we should cherish this long road
From very hazy beginnings
To a very definite end
Enjoy the trip around the next bend

Come Back To Me My Love

Where, oh! Where, oh! Where
Are you gone to
Where in the cosmos is your abode
For Heaven is an uncreated place
And you are living now in space

I feel you near, I feel you far
You live within the confines
Of a jar
Tumbling through the spatial inter dimension
You know the physics of life to its very end

So come back to me my love
And tell me all there is
The story of creation from first to last
The whispered dream you had
From God's awareness
So I too may dream a new reality

A Peeking Concentration

There is a simple thing you did
Which makes me laugh still
Poke you tongue through you teeth
To show a much determined will

Crosswords, simplex, sudoku
Were your empassioned train
Resolving to succeed in ways
To fortify your brain

Oh! How much you concentrated
Peeking through your teeth
That tongue of your's most natural
Gave glory to you always

Gathering Dust

I searched for my previous work
In the archive and found a treasure
Work I had forgotten
Just sitting there
Waiting to be found
And mined

For these were not the ramblings
Of a fool
They were put there by another being
In a heightened state of consciousness
A trove of knowledge
The beginnings of a book

So now it is time to lift them
Out of the history of their past
And transform them into
A reasonable tome

Otherwise they will gather dust
And never see the light of day
And that would be a pity
For pity it will not be
As I plant the knowledge tree

It's A Boy

Oh! Dearest love what can I say
I seem at a loss today
It is so short a time
To celebrate in rhyme
Your momentous undertaking

For you singularly achieved
The moment you delivered
A beautiful bouncing baby boy
Small enough to be a toy
What a great gift from God

Now grown large he make's his way
Through the world and has his say
He's become a man you see
Tall and strong he'll always be
What a beautiful, beautiful, beautiful boy

Time Flies

By god, this life is tenacious
Urging us on to live to the full
All the days that we have
Do not dally or dawdle
Kick the ball down the street
Be swift on your feet
Run as fast as you can
Hurry up
Don't be the man to be slow
It's hard to think that
Not even a month has passed
Since you died
I'm tongue tied

Mixed Messages

Dearest, dearest, dearest love
Why does it make no sense
Your gone from us
Now and forever
The living ties did sever

I feel like crying every day
But fight it the world away
The tears will do no justice
To your most august choice

Now that I'm feeling sad for you
And complex mishmash happy too
At least you didn't suffer
I offered as a buffer
To the pain of losing you

Moving On

It is time to consider the future
To adapt life to your passing
To effect a change in daily rhythms
To begin to live again

For we can only mourn for so long
Our awareness would not tolerate
A prolonged period of deep reflection
The tolling of a bell

So now my dear will I move on
To pastures new in life
Move on but ne'er forgetting
My glad and beauteous wife

A Loving Wife

I accept your loss within my life
My gracious and forgiving wife
Although together we would never be
I do not like to be living free

For you were then of much renown
To always smile and never frown
There is a sacred simple text
A prayer to God you'd say

Now deep within my own dear dream
I knew we'd make a living team
To bring in to the world of ours
A wonder to the lord, a boy

Now, that he's fully grown in life
Thinking 'tis time to get a wife
I ask you for the blessing day
With vows of love they both do say

To Sleep or Rest

When do we sleep, when do we rest
That is a question for the best
Now that you are gone
The difference is the same
For eternity there is a game
Of life
Now that I experience slumber
In the shadow of the dark
I feel the sorrow of your going
Deep within my heart
And wish you were only
Sleeping

The End Of Dreams

I wish that I could dream
So that all would seem
Well
Now that Heaven's door is open
I can look inside my dreams
To get a feeling of
The beauty of
This place
To conjure joy
It is a ploy
To fool myself that all is well
When it's not
As you are gone and never will
Return

Memories Of You

My dearest love you were my wife
My intimate partner in this life
No one else did touch my soul
As easily as you

For you were such a special being
A smiling spiritual freeing
Unencumbered was your day
And night you slumbered play

Now that you are gone from us
My heartstrings weep and willow
I dream your head upon my chest
A gently moving pillow

Oh! Now my dear I do accept
Your passing it is true
You lived a brilliant life for us
You ate the daily stew

Now once in motion I set my mind
These words I hope to do you kind
My memories precious are to me
I hang them on my wishing tree

Fulfilling Desire

Now I must fulfil your greatest desire
To be an active means of expression
To be a facility with words
To be the sound you cannot make

For you are silent now my love
Your voice will never more be heard
Your beautiful art serves as a legacy
Your friendliness revered by all

Oh! Dear love I miss you so
The end of the day especially
The end of the night I can endure
The end of your life it came so soon

Heaven's Door

Please let us signify the breaking day
The bloom of Heaven in a play
The garden of God displaying a flower
Consummate feeling with a bidding power
For we are animate you see
Fully alive and rarely free
This cosmic choice we have to make
Delivers our health for everyone's sake
And bids us dream forever more
In Heaven's place we have a door

A Rich Man

I am become my own true self
That's what he said
In the middle of our session
I am become the man I always was
Full of courage, kindness and love
Never lose that he said
It is worth the riches of the universe

Ageless Girl

Oh! Dearest, dearest, dearest girl
You are still just twenty years old to me
You are still in your late twenties just
When we got married
You are still in your early thirties
When Eoghan was born
You have not aged at all
And yet you have
You have reached an eternal age
You cannot get any older

A Cosmic Marriage

Now that I sit and ponder
On your life
Our life together was made in Heaven
We lived and loved as cosmic beings
Inheriting from God
The bliss of wedding bells
But reality came to soon
When we jumped over the moon
And landed in a crumpled ball
Tripped over life in a fall
And never recovered
For we were like so many
Able to love
But not suited to stay
Together
Now forever apart we will be
But in God's mind
Together and forever free

A Journey To Heaven

You know my dear I've shed a tear
For you every day of late
My mind is still getting used
To the loss of your life
You are gone from us
On a solo journey
To the other side of the universe
Started in a hearse
But now in a chariot of gold
For you are joined
To the Heavenly throng
An angel in mercurial dress

A Faint Memory

My dearest I must now be honest
I do not know where
That you've gone
I like to think you're in Heaven
But my heartstrings are doubting so
Your voice it grows as a stranger
Fainter by more everyday
Your face the image of beauty
Does dissolve like clouds in the sky
All that is left is a memory
A faint smile in the brightening day
And now that must content me
As I go about life as in play

A Melody Of Love

You sing forever in my heart
A love song that we shall never part
The glories of our lives to you
Shall echo in the chambers true
Now the day has come to say
The truth for all who hear what may
We never parted in our life
What e'er the turbulence and strife
A little break was all we needed
To heal the ground so lightly seeded
With love's flowers so soon to grow
A bunch of which I carry, though
You're gone forever now my dear
I'll lightly shed a little tear
Of love

A Deep Kingdom

There is a kingdom deep within my soul
Occupied by my queen of compassion
A deeply loving gentle girl
Full up with quiet talk

It's only on a silent day
Her gentle whisper I hear to pray
Murmuring tones a richness flows
With blissful exuberance it knows

The truth of everything it does tell
A fountain of knowledge deep as a well
So if you listen to your heart
She will do her part

And come to you

When Dreams Won't Come

What do I do when sleeping lie
Awake I cannot dream
My flitting mind is bubbling
With thoughts abounding still
I do not lay in slumber deep
No joyous blissful mood
Just constant interruptions
Which nightly fails to soothe
A listening to a heart beat
With rhythmic sounds abound
Will calm the mental anguish
Sufficient for to choose a way
To gently fall asleep

The Price Of Love

There's nothing in my head to write
No brilliant words of praise
Just honest phrases in my brain
A sequence, nay a train

'Tis painful when I seek to write
No noble thoughts do swell
For there is nothing in the dark
And swirling tumbling well

For now it seems my voice is quiet
My deep heart's silent too
Perhaps you've gone to sleep my love
Your words are glistening few

Now I wish to stop this pain
Emotions for to gain
A word or two will now suffice
To pay love's daily price

You Are Gone From Us

Now that you are gone from us
Your death it didn't cause much fuss
When tears were shed
We went to bed
And rose next day without you

For you are gone, we must obey
Life's dictum which is to pray
To Heaven's bells
With deeper wells
Of tears we have so many

Now that we've mourned your loss awhile
We faintly light a little smile
And get on through the day
A silent word we often say
To whisper in the wild

The trees are down upon their knees
A weeping willow sees
The truth is you will come again
To visit us
But when

Eternal Memory

My dearest love where are you gone
Where is your smile which beamed out so
We miss you of that I'm more than sure
The pain of loss is intimate and pure

Now that a month has passed since then
The day you awakened in an eternal glen
We're at a loss to know to do
A faint memory is all we have of you

So now I ask you to wait awhile
Linger in my mind and heart
For then I can do my part
And see you forever
'Till the end of time

Lost Letters

My dear the words go on their own
Like swords with no one to fight
Singular expressions of emotion
A lost labyrinth out of sight

We hear not all the feelings said
Deep down within a buried head
The lost souls do whisper out
An endless stream of Heaven's shout

For now I'll wander in the dust
These words with knowledge seeds and rust
Do potter in a quietened place
Blossoming in a sacred space

Now there is no meaning here
No advantage permanent and clear
I've foraged in my thoughts for joy
But they are lost for now
And ever

Just A Memory

To be honest is a way of life
A certain ruse to be forged
To hide within the confines
Of an uncreated play
The murmuring of this day
Does beckon to the lonely heart
The beating whispers of the fray
Lines up in fulsome memory
For you were once alive and true
A beautiful being of incandescent hue
Now you are but a memory
Etched in my numinous bone

A Monument To Life

When I was young my innocence was robbed
In a most regretful way
Not that I noticed
For I was innocent

But when
When did the certainty grow
When did the shame sow
Seeds of despair

There was a pair of them
They touched me
They touch me in my memory

But you were innocent of all this
Your innocence was infectious
It infected me with joy
I wish now it could be like a toy
And I a child playing

But no, such thoughts are not so simple
Parts of me wants a public display
A wall of names echoing the lost
Lost for a life time
What would it achieve I wonder
Such a monument to life

More Memories Of You

Opening the pages of memory
I search among half forgotten thoughts
Reminders of happy days
Sadness overwhelming too
Sifting with a well worn shoe
Kicking out the good and not so good
Enlivening life with every toe full
Glistening shining bright shining
Memories of a happy day
Now although not sad
They stop
And are replaced by the reality
You are gone
And memories are all we have

Faint Words Of Love

I find it much more of an effort
To find words in my heart
Words which express how I feel
My emotions are very settled
Not wild or sad
Not happy or mad
Just nestled in to the groove of life
Now that I have accepted your death
There is little I have to say
Except
Go well my love
Live your existence to the full
And make us proud

Last Words In Verse

Now that I must say goodbye to you
My love, my words are faint and few
There is a reticence in my verse
Emotions are grown terse
I do not wish to end
Words with meaning you'll tend
To grow in to great feeling
And let sadness graze the yellow saplings
For now everything comes to a stop
Great emotions laboured evermore
And a heart cushioned from every sore

Epilogue

Thank you for taking the time to read my poems, I hope that you enjoyed, at least some of them, as much as I enjoyed composing them. If you feel that you would like to write then I suggest that you begin with a very simple daily exercise, an exercise in writing. In polite company it is called 'morning pages.' Simply get an A4 sheet of paper and start writing, for twenty minutes in the morning, or another suitable time of the day. Don't worry about what you say, just get the pen to paper. Initially it is better to write rather than type, as paying attention to your penmanship is important. In less polite company, I call this, 'write the shite.' Write all the good, bad and indifferent stuff, then you will find your own voice. So best of luck writing. Let me know how you get on. My e-mail is at the beginning of the book.

Brian G

21-12-23

Printed in Great Britain
by Amazon